He was a fighter pilot in World War II. He was a pilot in the Korean war. In between, Ted Williams carved out one of the most remarkable baseball careers of all time.

The last man to hit .400 in a season, a ` man who created excitement and controversy through his actions on and off the field, Williams came up to 1957, age 39, fighting time—and a younger baseball idol named Mickey Mantle.

It was the most glorious fight of his career. Edwin Pope, Sports Editor of the Miami *Herald*, expertly captures that stirring head-to-head duel—Ted Williams vs. Mickey Mantle—for American League batting supremacy.

Here is Ted Williams' golden year with all its tensions . . . all its drama . . . and, finally, all its glory.

TED WILLIAMS

the golden year *1957*

Edwin Pope

MB
MANOR BOOKS, INC.

A Manor Book..............1972

This is the complete text of
the hardcover edition

Manor Books, Inc.
329 Fifth Avenue
New York, New York, 10016

Library of Congress Catalog Card Number: 70-93101

TED WILLIAMS

the golden year **1957**

Foreword

The most significant moment during all of the baseball
exercises in the spring of 1969 came late one afternoon in
the bucolic pasture used by the Washington Senators in
Pompano Beach, Florida. An old major league infielder,
now a coach for the Senators—Wayne Terwilliger is his
name—was acting as the batting practice pitcher. From the
miniscule slit trench the Senators call a dugout stepped a
tall man with a long neck, his cap pulled down tight on his
head, wagging a slender bat. He stepped into the batting
cage, scuffed his toes in the dirt to make himself
comfortable and took his stance to swing at the practice
pitches. Everybody on the field: players, writers, coaches,
and straggly fans stopped to look.

Theodore Samuel Williams, "The Kid," was officially
back in baseball after an absence of eight years. And

Terwilliger said he would have something to tell his grandkids—pitching to Williams.

Because Ted Williams bringing his bat around in a graceful arc is the ultimate symbol of baseball perfection, this little act of batting practice signified more to the game than his selection to manage the Senators.

It revived the glory of his Golden Year of 1957 when, at the age of thirty-nine, he batted .388. It made people remember that he was the last .400 hitter in the majors (.406 in 1941). Or that his lifetime batting average of .344 would have led the American League every year since 1961.

Yet these figures are insufficient in the perspective of the man as a force in baseball. Today's inquisitive generation can identify with this acerbic soul who won't wear a tie or attend social functions, and yet will take the trouble to find out the name of an old sportswriter he hasn't seen in twenty years so he can flatter the gent with an informal greeting (this happened in the spring of '69, too).

Ted Williams is a complicated man: irascible, charming, articulate, profane, friendly, hostile, absorbed, irreverent. Nobody realized this better than Edwin Pope, the sports editor and columnist of the *Miami Herald*, when Williams invited him a couple of years ago to be his companion on a fishing trip off the Florida Keys, where Ted has made his home. Ted was the perfect host, even cooking breakfast. But he also told Pope when to get up and what to do. In that episode, and in others over the years, he revealed himself to Pope and laid a personality base upon which the author could reconstruct this Golden Year.

Murray Olderman

Chapter One

"Ted Williams is a man of courage; he is a person; he is ever the master of a situation and never its slave."

Branch Rickey

Hitting the deck early never presented the problem to Theodore Samuel Williams that it has to so many others. With him it was more luxury than deprivation. Williams seldom could sleep past 6:30 A.M. anyway. It was infinitely more pleasant for him to be up and active than twisting and tumbling in his bed in the Ringling Hotel in Sarasota, Florida.

Restless and so very tense, with a mind as inquisitive as it was acquisitive, by seven-thirty he had wolfed down a breakfast of liver, bacon and a pair of lambchops. Then he was out walking or driving his Ford sedan through Sarasota's serene boulevards. When the sporting-goods stores opened, he talked fishing or baseball with shopkeepers he knew. Or if he chanced by a photographic studio that might have cracked its doors a trifle ahead of schedule, he might wander in and discuss exposures, light meters and such until it was time to check in at the tumbledown old Sarasota ballpark.

This was early March of 1957—the start of what was to be his golden year. Ted Williams was thirty-eight years old. He would turn thirty-nine on August 18. He had reached an age where most baseball players were either resting on their laurels or resting, period.

He could not possibly look ahead 12 years to the spring of 1969, when, astonishingly to all, including himself, he would be named manager of the Washington Senators. But he could look back.

Indeed he had far more to look back upon than any player of his generation.

Only major-leaguer in the past twenty-seven years to hit more than .400, with .406 in 1941. Twice Most Valuable Player in the American League (1946 and 1949). Four times named Major League Player of the Year (1941, '42, '47, and '49) by *The Sporting News*. Four times the American League's leading hitter (.406 in 1941, .356 in 1942, .343 in 1947 and .369 in 1948). Never a batting average lower than .318 in a full season since 1939 with the Boston Red Sox.

His greatness already had touched three decades. "And hell," he often reminded himself and any others within earshot, "if I really had been able to run, I think I could have broken a lot of Ty Cobb's records."

Running was the problem that looked largest in that 1957 spring. Never possessed of more than average speed even in the sunburst prime of his youth, Williams now had to have a very emphatic hit to reach first base. There would be no more "leg hits," the kind Willie Mays and Henry Aaron and Mickey Mantle and others like them achieved on sheer speed. This year would prove once and for all whether Williams' great forearms and wrists and reflexes could outpoint time, that cruelest rival of every athlete.

Ted had driven the 300-odd miles from his fisherman's home in Islamorada in the Florida Keys (picking up a traffic ticket or two along the way, since he usually drove as though he had illusions of prepping for the Indianapolis 500) to take his first workout in Sarasota.

As usual writers and photographers overwhelmed him. As usual they were unsure of what to expect. But they *were* sure that something newsworthy would emerge from the confrontation.

"Aren't you a little heavy?" one asked.

"Sure, I'm a little heavy," Williams said brusquely. "I'm always heavy this time of the year." His normal playing weight was about 198 pounds. "I'm 212 now, I guess," he said.

He grinned. That grin was something to see when he really wanted to turn it on; this time he did. His green eyes glinted—someone once called them "Lindbergh eyes." He asked the writers if they had talked over his training program with Manager Mike Higgins. "When you find out what it is," he said, "be sure and let me know what I'm supposed to do. I want you to be happy."

That was the first record set by Ted Williams in 1957, wanting Boston journalists to be happy.

This record was to be short-lived. By April he would have enveloped himself in heavy silence, refusing comment on almost everything. But these were the golden days of spring in Sarasota, by the Gulf of Mexico, where springs can be very very golden, and life looked pretty okay to the big guy.

"Listen, you Knights of the Keyboard!" he bellowed in the voice that could have passed for that of actor Cliff

11

Robertson. "You hear what I did to Ted Lepcio during the Sportsman's Show in Boston?"

Lepcio was a Red Sox infielder, and the Sportsman's Show was a perennial showcase for Williams' fly-casting abilities.

"I telephoned Lepcio," Williams explained, unable to smother his mirth, "and told him I was a baseball writer for United Press. I asked him if he had signed his contract and Lepcio said, 'No.' Then I asked him if he was a holdout, and Lepcio said he wasn't exactly a holdout either.

" 'Well, how about Ted Williams? Has Ted Williams signed?' I asked Lepcio then. And Lepcio said. 'Yes, sir, I understand the Red Sox floated a loan and signed him.'

"Then I thanked Lepcio and hung up, and I was busting a gut laughing."

Williams could afford to laugh. It was not true that the Red Sox had had to "float a loan" to sign him. Not with millionaire Tom Yawkey's money behind them. However, Ted certainly was in the $125,000-a-year class, although reportedly some of this was arranged as deferred payment. A more or less hand-to-mouth childhood as the son of a Salvation Army mother and a father of many jobs in San Diego was nothing more than an acid memory now.

Most of the writers ringing the batting cage in Sarasota called him "Ted" or "Williams" or just "No. 9." Time had charitably erased some of the early collection of awful nicknames that were hung about his neck like obnoxious albatrosses—"The Splendid Splinter," "Thumping Ted," "Terrible Teddy," "Titanic Teddy," "Terrific Ted," "Tarzan Ted," "Timely Ted" and so on *ad nauseum*. About the only name that stuck was "The Kid," the one that he resented the least and the one that was certainly far less fulsome than "Splendid Splinter," which later became "Splendid Spitter" when he expectorated in the direction of some Boston fans. Not on them, just at them.

Williams did not find the writers in the best of moods that spring, anyway.

12

For one thing, the club had only recently switched its spring headquarters from the Sarasota Terrace to the Ringling Hotel. From the Terrace, just above the ballpark, some writers could watch practices and exhibitions from the windows of their hotel rooms. But the Ringling was two miles away. Writers were forced to drive two miles to the park every day. One—Roger Birtwell of the *Boston Globe*—did not even own a car since he lived near a bus-line in Boston. The switch to the Ringling forced him to buy a car. Birtwell also swore that the *Globe*'s Harold Kaese, who never drove, wore out two pairs of shoes walking between the Ringling Hotel and the ballpark that spring.

Such were the circumstances that spring day in 1957 when Ted Williams stepped into the batting cage for his first swing of the year.

The writers stared in spite of themselves. They seldom could bring themselves to be blasé around No. 9. He either angered them or stirred them to the edge of hero-worship. But invariably he excited them and drew their undivided attention. Just looking at Williams was enough to bug out the eyes of the journalists.

He was 6 feet 4 inches tall. At thirty-eight, he had filled out more to the proportions of a professional football player than a baseball outfielder. Even as a young man, the almost invisibly quick flick of his wrists and the eyes that seemed to recognize every stitch of the ball had frightened pitchers enough. But in 1957 he had weight to go along with the hand-and-eye coordination so delicately matched as to command the envy of a championship golfer.

A jackhammer operator would have been proud to have Williams' hands, long and strong. His forearms were mindful of the trunk of a baby oak. And he was not fat, although thick-bodied.

The face that had been thin to the point of gauntness nearly two decades before had filled out into an image not unlike that of a more mature Rock Hudson. One watching

13

him in profile could see a certain resemblance to Ted's longtime hero, Gen. Douglas MacArthur—straight nose, out-thrusting chin and cheekbones. Ted Williams was and is an excessively handsome man. His whole being breathed forth a command presence. Long before he became manager of the Washington Senators in 1969, many questioned whether his emotional makeup was suitable for a successful manager. There never was an atom of doubt that Williams was always *in charge* as a player.

Branch Rickey, one of baseball's demigods, had said it well: "Ted Williams is a man of courage; he is a person; he is ever the master of a situation and never its slave."

This was what the men around the batting cage saw when Williams whipped his bat into a baseball for the first time in 1957.

The bat splintered.

That should have been the tipoff. A lot of things were going to break in front of Ted Williams in the next seven months.

He had no way of knowing it then. His winter had been routine—for him. Almost daily, from his fishing cottage on U.S. Highway No. 1 in the Florida Keys some eighty miles west of Miami, he had been out on the flats searching for bonefish or lying in wait for his favorite salt-water prey, the cunning tarpon Atlanticus.

He had even outfished his old buddy, golfer Sam Snead, in a special "fish-off" during the Metropolitan Miami Fishing Tournament. He had boated a pair of eight-pound bonefish to a single catch for Snead. Then, facetiously but not without a modicum of justification, he had reannounced himself as "still the world's No. 1 fisherman."

He had caught a cold, too. While he was supine and suffering, another old friend had dropped by. This was Fred Corcoran, a professional golfing pioneer who also served as Ted's business manager.

"Don't see why you got a cold now," Corcoran had said.

14

"Thought you only got one of those when the Cleveland Indians come to town and Herb Score is going to pitch."

Williams came out of his sickbed, expostulating in mock anger. "That's a lie! I do all right against Score. Just look at the records. Just because I had a cold one time last year when the Indians came to Boston . . ."

But they really were only joking. The next day, at his Keys home, Williams had himself another yuck. He read that Ty Cobb, the Georgia Peach who had torn up basepaths and baseball teams in the early part of the century, had criticized him for his off-season training methods.

"If Williams wants to go two or three more years," said the seventy-year-old Cobb from his home in Atherton, California, "he has to keep his legs in shape. The older you are, the harder you have to train.

"When I was a young fellow," Cobb went on. "I could be in shape after eight or nine days of training. Often, I could have played as soon as I reported. But in my later years I had to work hard for a month during spring training even though I always disciplined myself during the off-season by hunting and hiking. That's how I kept my legs ready at all times."

Cobb seemed to make a special project of Williams, more from fondness and admiration than enmity or envy. In 1946, when Manager Lou Boudreau of the Cleveland Indians installed the shift that moved almost the entire defense to the right side against the left-handed-hitting Williams, Cobb had warned Williams that he would be through as a top hitter unless he learned to hit to those open spaces in left field.

"Son, if you'd just hit to left," Cobb almost pleaded with Williams, "you'd crush every hitting record that was ever put in a book. I'd even say you could hit .500."

Instead, Williams had accepted the challenge of the Boudreau Shift. Doubtless it cost him hits. But Ted's

15

natural virtuosity enabled him to lead the American League in 1947 with .343 and in 1948 with .369. He hit .343 again in 1949 before an elbow injury in the 1950 All-Star game restricted him to 89 games and a .317 average.

Thus the old Georgia Peach's 1957 wintertime jab at Williams' training regimen, or lack of it, had given Ted little concern.

"You try some of that standing up in a boat all day, and then poling the boat around those flats out there in the Keys," said Williams, "and you'll see what kind of shape you get in.

"Hell's bells, I never bought that stuff about a guy having to torture himself into condition during the off-season. The thing is, you shouldn't ever get *out* of shape. If you don't drink, if you don't smoke, if you don't eat yourself out of house and home, and if you don't stay up all night raising cain, just your ordinary activities will keep you in shape.

"I didn't play any baseball or get a chance to do any training for baseball when I was in service the first time in 1943 and 1944 and 1945, did I?" he demanded. "And what did I do when I came back in 1946?"

What he had done in 1946 was lead the Red Sox to their first pennant in twenty-eight years, hit .342, 38 home runs, bat in 123 runs and get himself named Most Valuable Player in the American League.

"I sure as hell didn't play any baseball when I was flying Marine planes in Korea in 1952 and 1953, did I?" Ted went on. "And what did I do when I came back in 1954?"

What he had done in 1954 was punch out a .345 average, 29 home runs and bat in 89 runs.

"So," he concluded, "you can take that stuff about off-season conditioning and . . . well, forget it.

"Besides, our Ted Williams Tackle Manufacturing Company just had the best year it ever had. I can't very well ignore that, can I? During season I work on baseball. I don't think there's anybody today—or anybody ever—who worked harder at hitting than I do. So when the season's over, I do what I please and I keep in shape my own way. And that ought to be the end of that."

Not everyone can condone some of the things Ted Williams did in baseball, such as the obscene gesture to fans and the spitting incident in 1950, or the spitting performance in 1956 ("hydrotheatrics," one pundit called it) that got him fined $5,000 by Red Sox general manager Joe Cronin. But there were times when Williams' peevishness with the press seemed to have a point.

In the greatest season of his life, 1941, he had lost the MVP title to Joe DiMaggio because DiMag uncurled a 56-game hitting streak that year. And in the 1957 season now approaching, an episode of remarkably similar nature was to occur.

Harold Kaese of the *Boston Globe* had given the other side of this much-bandied Williams-press feud in *Sport Magazine* when he wrote:

A writer *could* compose something nice about Williams every day, but it would get very monotonous and, as far as reporting went, dishonest. It is an inner compulsion to be honest that makes some writers present the seamy side of life, and some others the shortcomings of potent personalities like Williams. Such writers are often charged with picking on Williams, as if they are innately cruel.

Obviously, it is wrong to distort any man's character. But because it is more repulsive to distort it in the direction of the bad does not mean that it is of little significance to distort it in the direction of the good. Too often great athletes are glorified and falsified for no good reason and to no good purpose, but there are always opportunists ready to meet the demand for heroes.

Ted Williams can't be left alone any more than a Harry Truman, a Dwight Eisenhower, an Albert Einstein or a Frank Sinatra can be left alone. He means much to society, and society has the right to know him—as he is, not as the sycophants would like us to have him.

You may say that is another story entirely. It is not. Not at all. Much of what Williams achieved and said or did not say in 1957 traced directly to (1) his outspokenness and (2) his anger over having some supposedly private comments about the Marine Corps, President Truman and Sen. Robert Taft and "gutless politicians" published. He had believed the comments were made in confidence. They turned out to be anything but confidential.

However, this happened later, and now we are with Teddy Ballgame, his ironic and favorite self-appellation, in spring training camp in Sarasota in 1957.

Higgings was the Red Sox manager then; he had been since 1955. Soft-spoken, understanding, he got along with Williams. But then Ted had gotten along well enough with all his other major-league managers—Joe Cronin (1939-47), "a great guy and a great manager to talk hitting with"; Joe McCarthy (1948-50), "the best manager I ever played for"; Steve O'Neill (1950-51) and Lou Boudreau (1952-54); whom Williams delighted in calling "The Frenchman."

"Ted looks good, doesn't he?" Higgins said in Sarasota. "He doesn't look heavy to me. And he's swinging as good as ever. I'd say he's in the best shape in years. I think he's going to take a shot at a special kind of season."

That was not what Williams was thinking. His thoughts centered on making this his last year. "I just hope I can start 100 games, and maybe play in 125, and hit .325 or a little higher," he said.

"If anybody had even asked me three years ago if I

18

would be in uniform in 1957, I'd have had to say no. Sometimes, I guess, when you think you're beginning to slip, you feel like packing up your bag and saying the hell with it. But when you get older, you think better of the game."

"What about your shoulder?" someone asked Williams. He had had trouble with it off and on since sustaining a broken collarbone in spring training of 1954. A stainless-steel pin had been inserted, and it was still in there in 1957.

Williams shrugged. "Yeah, the shoulder bothers me. But not in games, unless it's cold. When it really bothers me is at night, for some reason. And my elbow still gets stiff, too."

Neither showed in the daytime. March 2, four days after reporting, Ted bet Red Sox traveling secretary Tom Dowd he would hit a pitch over the Sarasota park's right-field fence, a distant 375 feet from home plate. Dowd took the bet. Williams promptly knocked two out of sight.

Just about then, some seventy miles cross-state in Lakeland, a twenty-two-year-old chap in Detroit Tiger clothes was explaining his feelings about Ted Williams. "When I was a rookie in 1953," said Al Kaline, "I was skinny as a rail. I went up to Ted and asked him for any help he could give me. Tell you the truth, I was so in awe of him, I almost backed down at the last minute. But I went on and asked him anyway.

"Ted told me I wasn't strong enough, which I already knew, but he gave me some advice on how to build myself up. It may sound simple now, but nobody else ever bothered to tell me the same thing. He just told me to get myself a couple of handballs and keep them with me all the time and keep squeezing them every time I could possibly think of it."

Kaline did that little thing. One year later he won the American League batting championship with .340—

youngest ever to do it, at twenty. (He was one day younger than Ty Cobb had been when he did the same thing in 1907.)

Kaline, in fact, attempted to ape Williams' hitting style to the extent that he was called "the right-handed Williams." Later Ted pointed out to the youngster, "You're not getting your pitches." Kaline, said Williams, was striking at what the *pitcher* wanted him to swing at, and not what Kaline should have been swinging at. Al quit biting on so many first pitches and/or bad pitches.

"I just wish I could hit the way Ted can," said Kaline, echoing thousands of other big-leaguers past and present. "He's the best. And one of the reasons is that he knows what's going on up at the plate at all times."

Back in Sarasota, Red Sox trainer Jack Fadden agreed. Fadden had been around the team a long time. He was closer to Williams than anyone else except clubhouse men Johnny and Vinnie Orlando. "Ted is a smart guy," Fadden explained. "He realizes the competition is getting tougher every year and he's getting older. That puts a double squeeze on him. He doesn't want to take any chances of slipping. He's very proud."

During Fadden's brief peroration, his subject was doing fifty repetitions of an exercise with a 25-pound weight. Then he dropped to the floor for fifty fingertip pushups.

By March 6, teammate Jimmy Piersall had signed his contract and posed for pictures with Williams to squelch rumors of a feud between the two. And Ted had pared down to little more than 200 pounds—hitting weight!

The next day brought a somewhat comic surprise to the Red Sox billet. The world's largest electronic computer, in Detroit, predicted Mickey Mantle of the Yankees would win the American League batting championship with a .342. The machine declared, clickety-clackety-clack, that Williams would finish second at .322. Ted laughed. He did not base his hitting on what came out of a computer, although he conceded that his own work with the bat had a consistency which might lend itself to analysis by computer.

He was not playing as the Red Sox opened the Grapefruit League season. He seldom played this early in the year. Indeed, much of his spring-opening activity consisted of signing autographs for pop-eyed tykes who swarmed the Sarasota park.

Today Williams will recall the "awful boredom" of spring games, but he believes that the early part of every season was the key to the entire year.

"Every year that I got off to a good start, I generally ended up with a hell of a record," he said. "Every year that I got off poorly, I'd end up with an ordinary record, for me. My record is so consistent it's pretty near monotonous.

"I've never had many real dips. The first two weeks and the last two weeks were my trouble areas. It was so cold and damp and windy at those times. I'm a hot-weather guy. I never got beat-down from the heat. It just loosened me up and made me feel more like playing. Matter of fact, I always felt I had an advantage over pitchers because I could stay strong longer than they could. Pitchers lose more than hitters do when the thermometer starts rocketing up there.

"In cold weather, in the spring and fall, particularly in a place like Boston, the ―――― pitchers have all the advantage. They wrap up in jackets and electric blankets during games, and they're warmed up even before that. They don't get frozen up like the hitters do."

Part of this early-March period, when Williams was not playing, he would leave the park and go back to the Ringling Hotel and tie fishing flies.

He had no roommate. "It wasn't fair to me, because I liked privacy, and it wasn't fair to a roommate, because the telephone was always ringing for me," he said with Williamsesque candor.

Nor was he a lobby-sitter like Al Lopez or Tony Cuccinello or so many old-timers. "First of all, I couldn't stand people gawking at me in the lobbies. So I'd either ride around town or go fishing with a friend of mine who had a boat and two nice kids, and we'd go out and catch tarpon or snook or whatever. Then at night I'd mostly walk around Sarasota. In the early years, first when Bobby Doerr and later when Billy Goodman was on the club, we'd walk three or four miles, looking in storewindows, talking hitting, just bulling, you know, just killing time until ten-thirty or so, and then I turned in. But after Goodman left I sort of kept to myself. That included walking by myself."

Plainly the motive behind some of his nocturnal pedestrianism was to get away from the hordes of writers who trailed the Red Sox. He had made a recent statement similar to so many others in his career in that it led him back into hot water. "The Yankees will win the pennant," Ted had said. "They won it last year without much trouble, nine games over Cleveland, and they should be better after picking up Bobby Shantz and Art Ditmar. We haven't helped ourselves, that I can see. I don't think we can expect to be any better than fourth again, since we'll be playing with the same personnel."

This was to prove remarkably accurate. The Yankees won that 1957 pennant, and the Red Sox finished third. But reaction to Williams' original statement was severe.

Is he throwing in the sponge already? How can you win if you don't think you're going to win? What is he, some kind of defeatist?

Williams answered that that was the way he looked at it, realistically, and just to check the standings at the end of the year although, the Lord knows, he wanted to win the championship worse than anything because he might not have many more chances.

Funny thing was, a former Red Sox slugger and Hall of Famer had said the same thing, except more so, about the same time Williams had. That was old Jimmy Foxx (remember the joke around Boston: how does Foxx pronounce the second *x?*), who added without conspicuous diplomacy: "And if it wasn't for Williams, the Red Sox would be almost hopeless."

Foxx had had his say-so in Manchester, New Hampshire, after a New York columnist had written that the Red Sox would never win another pennant as long as Williams played for them.

"Well, where would the Red Sox be without Williams?" asked Foxx in rebuttal. "He's still a great hitter. He hasn't hurt the Red Sox any. If they didn't have Ted coming back, they wouldn't have a chance for the first division. Even with him, they're going to have a tough time making it."

A rumor spread on March 11, 1957, during the Red Sox' 2-0 exhibition loss to the Yankees, that AL President William Harridge was upset about Williams' talk about the Yankees being shoo-ins. But Harridge did not remonstrate with Williams.

In this case the Biblical injunction "This, too, shall pass" held true. But it was not always so with Ted Williams.

Two days later Ted still was inactive but had an opportunity to renew acquaintances with Stan Musial during a Grapefruit game with the St. Louis Cardinals. This was a classic meeting. They were the two finest hitters of the era, and most other eras as well. A continuous controversy was carried on over which was better.

"It was always that way," Williams mused. "It was Williams against Greenberg, or Williams against DiMaggio, or Williams against Musial, or Williams against What's-His-Name? I was always having to stand off somebody, so I must have been able to do something with the bat."

23

There never appeared to be any jealousy between Williams and Musial. Early in 1957, though, both were getting a bit long in the tooth: Williams was thirty-eight and Musial was thirty-six. They chatted casually for ten minutes and agreed on two things.

"Doubleheaders are getting to be pure torture for me," said Musial.

"Same here," Williams replied. He added, "You know, Stan, I think we both can still see and hit the ball as good as ever. But the legs . . ."

It was Musial's time to nod.

The 1957 exhibition season began for Williams on March 17. The Red Sox were playing the Brooklyn Dodgers in Miami, where Williams made his home off and on and operated his fishing-tackle business. He regarded Miami as a semi-home town and wanted to perform before the 7,876 who had come to plush Miami Stadium in the hope of seeing him.

So manager Higgins put him in left field for three innings against the Dodgers. The first time up he doubled off Bob Darnell, whistling the ball into left-center. He was picked off second base a few moments later. His next two times up he walked, then took a seat on the bench the rest of the evening. But his presence in the lineup, if ever so briefly, must have meant something to the Red Sox. Going into that exhibition, they had scored only eight runs in 58 innings. They beat the Dodgers, 9-4.

If ever a man's first hit of a spring was saturated with portent, that one was.

A little more into March brought a near-historic conference in Sarasota which touched upon Williams at least in a tangential way. Hank Greenberg, Cleveland general manager, was in town. Joe Cronin, Greenberg's opposite number with the Red Sox, promptly offered Greenberg a flat 1 million dollars for Herb Score, his twenty-two-year-old left-handed smokeballer.

Cronin was not kidding.

That jacked up a few eyebrows. Oh sure, snickered some critics, Score had had two big starting seasons. But a million dollars for a kid with only two years of big-league experience? Baloney, and double baloney!

Williams did not say anything about baloney. He said he thought Score would have been a bargain at a million dollars.

"Herb's worth a million . . . easy," said Ted. "Any guy who strikes out 245 men in one season and comes back with 263 more the next year . . .

"Listen, this kid can be better than Hal Newhouser. Not even Newhouser ever struck out that many. Except for Bob Feller's 348 whiffs back in 1946, Score's 263 was the highest strikeout total since old Walter Johnson fanned 303 back in 1912."

Williams deserted statistics for a few seconds. "Score's got better stuff than Newhouser," he said without equivocation. Then he went back to figures. "Why, Score ought to win 280 games before he finishes . . . *if he doesn't get hurt. . . .*"

That "if" was to haunt Williams in the most melancholy way less than two months later, when Score was struck in the eye by a drive off Gil McDougald's bat. Score kept trying to play until 1962 but won only fifteen more games after 1957 and finally had to give it up altogether in '62.

Williams never stopped regarding Score's injury as one of the gravest personal tragedies of his own era.

On March 20 the Red Sox headed for California and some exhibition action there. For once Ted was steamed up about a preseason game. His mother, May, who never had seen her son in a major-league game, finally was going to get a chance. And Ted could not but have reflected at the time on a childhood in which he developed traumas that had the most severe sort of bearing on his conduct throughout his life.

He disliked then, and dislikes to this day, discussing those days except to call them "unhappy." His mother was so devoted to her work with the Salvation Army that she was known as the "Angel of Tijuana." She was with the Salvation Army for almost fifty years at bases ranging from San Diego to Honolulu. Often, when she made street appearances with the Salvation Army band, little Teddy was expected to be there. He was made miserable by this requirement, ever fearful of being seen by young friends.

"To my mother's dying day, I never got over it," said Williams, "although I sure loved and respected her for everything she did for me and so many other people."

But his mother was, after all, toiling on behalf of people's souls for an inordinate number of hours per day. She wasn't home as much as some mothers, through no fault of her own. "I remember the house was dirty all the time," Williams once said with some distaste, his eye sweeping inadvertently across his own spotless home in the Florida Keys. And his father usually was busy at a photographic shop in downtown San Diego or at some other job. Ted's only brother, Danny, was, in Ted's own words, "always in some sort of scrape."

Baseball was Ted's way out, little though he knew it at the time. He was an indifferent student except for history and typing. He was not particularly interested in girls, mostly because he was so shy.

Only baseball.

He got to school before anybody else. "I wanted to be there when the janitor opened the baseball supply-closet before school," he explained.

As a pitcher and outfielder, he hit .583 and .406 for his final two seasons at San Diego's Hoover High. He also pitched for American Legion Post No. 6.

One day, one of his hits broke a window in a nearby home. That night, remembers Forrest Warren, a San Diego newspaperman who knew the Williams family, two men came to the Williams house. Both Ted and his mother thought they were policemen seeking restitution for the shattered window.

"Tell them a straight story," his mother instructed him, "and if they want $10 for the window . . . well, I'll get it somewhere."

The two men were not policemen. They were baseball scouts. One was Bill Essick of the Yankees. He wanted to sign Ted, then only seventeen. Ted's mother asked for a $1,000 bonus. Too much, said Essick, in one of the most short-sighted judgments in sports history. Essick went away and did not come back.

Thereupon Mrs. Williams signed for her son with Bill Lane, owner of a new Pacific Coast League franchise in San Diego. Young Ted was to receive $150 a month with the additional stipulation that he would not be traded until he was at least twenty-one years old, and that if he were sold to the big leagues, Mrs. Williams would receive 10 percent of the selling price.

In two seasons in San Diego, Ted hit .271 and .291. Nothing special, those averages, but the second year he hit 23 home runs, and that was 23 more than he had hit in his first professional season.

Meanwhile, the Red Sox had taken an option to buy young Williams for $25,000. That was how he landed in Minneapolis in the American Association in 1938 for a stormy season under Donie Bush, and graduated to Boston in 1939—and seldom went home again.

Chapter Two

"I used to respect Senator Taft . . . but he was just a gutless politician. A friend of mine was recalled for Korea. He knew Senator Taft. He asked Taft to help him get deferred. Do you know what Taft told my friend? Taft said, 'I can't touch you. You're pretty well-known where you live. If you were just another guy, I'd be able to help you.' Now do you know why I think politicians are gutless?"

Ted Williams

Now Ted Williams was heading back to what, although it never had been exactly the home he wanted, was at least the place where he had grown up.

He admitted he was looking forward to it. It would be the first time he had played in San Diego in sixteen years, when he had been a part of Jimmy Foxx's barnstorming troupe after the 1941 season.

Ted meandered into an exclusive haberdashery in San Francisco on March 23. He was going to buy a sports jacket; at least, if he never wore neckties, he condescended to don a jacket now and then. A clerk was fitting him out when an earthquake hit San Francisco. It brought the city's worst tremors since 1906.

"Cripes, it stopped me in my tracks," Williams says today. "The tailor was trembling so much he couldn't even go on with the measurements. The whole shop was shaking like it was going to cave in any minute, and people were running up and down the streets outside hollering bloody murder.

"I guess they had plenty to be scared about, the people that had lived in San Francisco all their lives and knew what an earthquake could do. I wasn't really all that up on earthquakes.

"I won't say I was downright scared but I guarantee you I was apprehensive. I'd never been through anything even close to something like that. It sounded like a thunderclap, only about twenty times louder . . . more like a sonic boom, I'd say from my flying days . . . and clothes were jiggling around the haberdashery like feathers in a blizzard. Then we had eight more shocks within the next seventeen hours.

"It wasn't the kind of thing that would get you 'up' for a ballgame."

That it did not. The Red Sox lost 2-1 to the San Francisco Seals and, incidentally, to a Red Sox rookie farmhand named Earl Wilson although Williams had a single in three times at bat.

Two days later he stroked his first exhibition homer as the Sox beat their San Francisco farmhands, 3-0. A total of 57,376 had seen the three games, of which Williams had played in two.

After all his emotional anticipation of the return to San

Diego, Williams' mother was ill and unable to see him play on March 27. At least that was one story. Some said that Mrs. Williams was on hand but was tucked away in a corner of the stadium so that she would not be bothered by reporters. Ted himself says she was not there and lets it go at that.

But things were popping as usual around Teddy Ballgame. He had been playing so little that writers were speculating that he would be of small use during the regular season. For the first time in 1957, Williams expressed himself on his playing prospects. "I'm going to play a lot more than you think." he told the newspapermen. "You——forget that once I started playing last year, I didn't miss a game."

They had only to check the records to verify that. Once in full harness in 1956, Williams had played in 136 games, batting .345 and hitting 24 home runs with 82 runs batted in.

Williams' earlier estimate of Herb Score was borne out in ironic fashion when the Red Sox faced the Indians in another exhibition on March 28. Score becalmed the Red Sox, 7-1, and Boston's only run came on Ted's homer.

"I could hit Score because basically he was my kind of pitcher," Ted would explain. "The guys that challenged me, I always could do all right against. It was the cuties and the people who kept the ball low and outside that bothered me.

"Score always pitched me high and tight . . . in here." He used his right hand to describe a rectangle starting about his forehead, going out perhaps a foot and down to the bottom of his chest, then back into the body.

"His fastball was tremendous and you know I could hit the hell out of fastballs. Generally I knew . . . and don't ask me how I knew . . . when he was going to try to overpower me, and I was ready for him.

"I'll tell you this. The way Score threw the ball, with that

30

fantastic velocity, if you ever did get a piece of it, it really flew out of there."

The Day, though, was yet to come. The Day was March 31. It had so little to do with baseball, yet so much to do with Williams' career. The episode was disconnected from baseball and at the same time became very much a part of it.

Certainly The Day turned Theodore Samuel Williams into something close to a recluse for the remainder of the 1957 season. Just as surely it broadened both the gaps of empathy and credibility between Williams and sports journalists—gaps already approximating the distance from the farthest corner of the Grand Canyon to the nearest.

On The Day, a sportswriter named Hy Hurwitz from the *Boston Globe* introduced Williams to one Crozet Duplantier, sports editor of the *New Orleans States*. The Red Sox had stopped in New Orleans on their way back to Florida. Hurwitz was a former Marine as was Williams and, as it turned out, so was Duplantier.

According to the best evidence, sports editor Duplantier asked Williams to say something in behalf of the Marine reserves. Williams did that and more. But ever after he insisted he was speaking off the cuff, that he met Duplantier only as a fellow ex-Marine and not as a newspaperman and that he had no intention that his remarks be made public.

Duplantier promptly returned to his paper and wrote a story quoting Williams as criticizing the Marine Corps, former President Harry Truman, Sen. Robert Taft and "gutless politicians" in general.

Williams said he had asked the Senator to intercede so that he would not be recalled in 1952, and that Taft had told him he (Williams) was too big for him to help in any way.

"If they had called back everyone in the same category as me, I'd have no beef," said Williams. "But they didn't.

They picked on me because I was well-known.

"I used to respect Senator Taft . . . but he was just a gutless politician. A friend of mine was recalled for Korea. He knew Senator Taft. He asked Taft to help him get deferred. Do you know what Taft told my friend? He said, 'I can't touch you. You're pretty well-known where you live. If you were just another guy, I'd be able to help you.' Now do you know why I think politicians are gutless?"

Baseball's Establishment was profoundly disturbed, from Commissioner Ford Frick on down to the lowliest club general manager. No less so was Williams. He said Duplantier had been drinking at the time of the interview.

But he did not deny the remarks.

Indeed, the very next day he snapped back with another slap at the government for its treatment of former heavyweight champion Joe Louis.

"Look at the terrible treatment Louis is getting," said Williams. "Here's a guy who has been a credit to his race and to his country. . . . I think it's a shame the way he's being hounded for his back income taxes. He'll never be able to pay all that money he owes the government. He's stuck for life. The interest keeps climbing every year and there isn't a damned thing he can do about it."

Meanwhile, a reaction came even from former President Truman in New York. "I'm not upset," said Truman, who had often advised people who could not stand the heat to stay out of the kitchen. "Williams is a great ballplayer and I like to watch him."

Later, however, Truman added, "The best way to get headlines is to attack a public figure, and if the public figure attacks back, then you get two headlines. Nobody can say anything about me that hasn't already been said."

Williams did not find himself friendless in the matter.

Joe Reichler, the scholarly and energetic journalist who went on to direct public relations for the baseball commissioner's office, was the reigning baseball expert for

The Associated Press when Williams sounded off in New Orleans. Reichler was waiting in Sarasota when the Red Sox returned to their training camp.

Reichler found Williams in the whirlpool bath in trainer Jack Fadden's inner sanctum. Reichler barged in without invitation. They had been friends for so long that some reporters referred to Reichler as "No. 9-1/2," a takeoff on Williams' famous No. 9 jersey.

"I might have known you'd be here, Bush," said Williams. "But you might as well go on back to St. Petersburg. I'm not talking to anybody."

"Oh, you'll talk to me, Bush," Reichler said airily. "Somebody's got to get you out of this mess."

Williams laughed. "And I suppose you're the guy to do it."

"Yes," said Reichler, "I am."

And Williams did talk. He proceeded to repeat his denunciation of Marine Corps policies, Truman, Taft, the whole works.

"Ted's bitterness," Reichler recalled in *Sport Magazine,* "was even more pronounced than in the New Orleans interview."

Reichler was not surprised. "I had been at the Jacksonville (Florida) Naval Base in April of 1952 when Williams was mustered into the Marines for the second time.

"When we went there, we weren't sure Williams would be accepted for service. The uncertainty stemmed from Ted's 1950 elbow fracture and, when Ted arrived at the Jacksonville base, a doctor took X-rays of the elbow."

Reichler went on: "Jerry Coleman of the Yankees was there, too. There was no doubt about him. He was in perfect health with no physical handicaps. We waited in an anteroom—Williams, Coleman, a couple of Boston newspapermen and I—for the results of the negatives. A Marine lieutenant told me it would be at least a half-hour before the pictures would be ready.

"The door opened and a Marine captain walked into the room," Reichler continued. " 'Congratulations, Capt. Coleman and Capt. Williams,' he said. 'The U.S. Marines are happy to have you aboard.'

"I was shocked. It was still 25 minutes or more before the negatives could be ready. I mentioned that to the captain. He shrugged. With more temper than tact, I questioned aloud the Marines' real purpose in recalling baseball's biggest name.

" 'The Marines don't really expect a thirty-three-year-old guy with four dependents to fly a plane?" I asked.

" 'I'm thirty-five with five dependents and I fly a plane,' the captain answered calmly."

Reichler pointed out that Williams went on to fly 39 missions in F-9 Panther jets in Korea. "Until his popoff in New Orleans," said the AP writer, "Ted never uttered any complaints. He kept his bitterness locked in his heart but he always felt that he would not have been recalled by the Marines if his name had been Joe Doakes instead of Ted Williams."

Now Williams was right back where he had been less than a year ago after The Great Expectoration—in hot water with press, public and baseball's higher authority.

He mended one fence by telegraphing an apology to Gen. Randolph Pate, Marine Corps commandant. "Four of the finest years of my life were spent in the Marine Corps," he wired Pate, and apologized for any unfavorable inference that might be drawn as to his opinion of the men of the Marine Corps.

Somehow the New Orleans incident seemed to revitalize Williams. He believes this was a supreme factor in his success during the season.

"Every time something came out about me that I thought was unfair or prejudiced, or just a plain lie," he said, "it always seemed to boost me up and I'd start hitting like crazy. For some strange reason, any troubles I had off the field helped my playing."

Certainly Williams' play was not hurting. On April 7 he was three for three in an exhibition against the Chicago White Sox. His streak moved him to tell Jim Piersall, "I feel so good I wish the season opened tomorrow."

Then, in one of his rare post-March utterances to Boston writers that year, he blurted, "You guys don't think I'll hit this year, but I will!"

Off his record to that time, there was little reason to doubt him. Williams had hit .324 for the exhibition season. He was the only Sox over .300 in the spring. But the very next day, just before homering against the Philadelphia Phils, Williams reversed his verbal field and picked Mantle, Kaline and Harvey Kuenn as the top three candidates for the 1957 American League batting championship.

Williams hit three more home runs before the season opened. One came on the field, against the Phillies. The other two were off the field.

He donated a color television set to Boston's Jimmy Fund Hospital, his favorite charity; and he actually wore a necktie as master of ceremonies at a Variety Club dinner honoring Red Sox owner Tom Yawkey.

And the season was ready to start.

Chapter Three

"I remember the first time I ever saw Ted Williams. It was 1938 and we were both in the Pacific Coast League, me with San Francisco and Ted with San Diego. I was sitting beside our manager, Lefty O'Doul, in the dugout watching Ted take batting practice. Lefty took one look at Ted and turned to me and said, 'There's the next Babe Ruth.' And Lefty O'Doul was the greatest hitting teacher I've ever known."

Dominic DiMaggio

As murderous as he was with bat on all occasions, Ted Williams was lethality personified in season-opening games. For thirteen major-league openers in which he played, his average was an electrifying .449.

Going into the 1957 opener before 38,227 spectators in Baltimore on April 16, he had hit in twelve consecutive openers.

Baltimore was not an easy place for Ted to hit the long ball. It was 370 feet down his power-alley to right-centerfield. But he jammed a home run in there against Bill Wight as the Red Sox won the opener, 4-2.

A day off led the Sox back to Fenway to open against the Yankees on April 18, and Williams pecked Johnny Kucks for two singles. Ironically, rightfielder Gene Stephens, later to become known as Williams' "caddy" because he replaced him so frequently for defensive purposes in late innings, blew the game for the Sox, 3-2, when he lost Gil McDougald's pop fly in the sun for a triple.

The auspicious early start for Williams had a solid foundation, even if he did not realize it at the time.

"I can see now what happened that spring," Ted will say today, "but I never mentioned it to anyone. Early in camp at Sarasota, I started to pick up a 34-1/2-ounce bat, where I ordinarily used a 33-ounce job early. It was odd, since I'd gotten into the habit of going with a lighter bat early in the year, but this big bat felt good. I mean, I was *ringing* the ball with it. Boom, right through the middle most of the time!

"As we started back north to open the season, I started going to the bat-rack for some of those lighter bats I'd always used. Then I said the devil with it, as long as I was going so good with the big one, I might as well keep on with it a little longer. I did. It was like it had iron in it.

"So I started the season with the big bat, and I never hit the ball any consistently harder than that year.

"I know why. The big bat was just perfect against the Boudreau Shift."

The Boudreau Shift, bane of Williams' existence for so long, had been originated in 1946 when the Red Sox were playing Lou Boudreau's Cleveland Indians.

Boudreau described the shift in his book, *Lou Boudreau, Player-Manager:*

> The Shift . . . consisted of swinging virtually all our defensive strength around to the right side of the diamond.

> I stationed the first baseman and the rightfielder virtually on the right-field foul line, moved the second baseman over much closer to first and back on the grass, placed myself to the right of second base, and ordered the third baseman to operate directly behind second.

> The centerfielder moved far to the right, taking care of the area normally patrolled by the rightfielder, and only the leftfielder remained to cover the vast expanse of open territory in left field.

But Williams was wrecking the shift as the 1957 season got under way.

"I started hitting the ball up the middle and to left," Ted said. "My hits were going through the hole where the shortstop would normally be if they didn't overshift to the right. Then they started shifting back toward shortstop a little bit, kind of opening up on me, for the first time in, hell, I guess more than ten years.

"I think everybody decided that since I'm hitting to left field pretty good now, I can't pull the ball to right anymore. Then they open up and I'm going good, and then I switch to a little bat.

"Where I hadn't been getting hits between first and second, now I'm getting them. If you went to right against a full shift, you'd have to be hitting a pea to find a hole for it to go through.

"That was the beginning of the breakthrough for me."

Most distracting of all to Williams was the shortstop's stratagem of standing behind a Red Sox runner on second base, and moving around, when a right-hander was pitching.

"You see," Ted said, "the shortstop would get right in line with the runner and the right-hander's arm, and it gave you a lot of irritating motion as a hitting background. So I'd tell Pete Runnels, 'If you get to second base, don't move too much, get your lead and stop so the shortstop has to stand still.' When that shortstop moved, it was about like having the fence moving on you. The effect was the same as far as hitting background was concerned."

The Red Sox lost a second game to the Yankees, 10-7, in Fenway Park on April 20 when Hank Bauer homered with a man on in the twelfth inning. But Williams' day included a double and two singles.

His second home run, and another single, came the next time out against the Yankees and Tom Sturdivant. The home run tied the score at 1-1 in the sixth on the way to Boston's eventual 5-4 triumph.

The single was a line job off the centerfield wall, a 420-foot shot that was one of the longest one-base hits on record. The ball had such velocity that the centerfielder took it on a quick bounce off the wall. It was hit *too hard*. The paradox was compounded by the fact that Sturdivant, a right-hander who eventually compiled a 59-51 record with six teams in the big leagues, was a passingly difficult man for Williams to handle.

"His ball was alive," said Ted. "And it moved a little bit, although he certainly wasn't overpowering. Anybody whose pitch was alive and moving was a lot tougher for me than a straight-ball pitcher no matter how hard the straight-ball guy threw."

By now, just four games into the '57 schedule, Williams was averaging .423. He pinged a double against Baltimore on April 22. He was two-for-four, including the 420th home run of his career, against the Orioles' Billy Loes on April 23. He caught a low inside delivery from Loes and deposited it 430 feet away in Fenway's centerfield bleachers in the first inning.

It should be pointed out here that many of the comments by Williams concerning the 1957 season actually were made much later, some as late as 1969 in conversations with the author. In 1957 Ted had drawn a veil over his off-the-field life and was speaking to practically no one except his closest friends.

Just why he was bending such efforts to keep his private life a secret is a good question, because it was anything but spectacular. But L'Affaire New Orleans had re-embittered him to the degree that he ducked not only writers but almost everyone as often as possible.

He had been divorced the year before from Doris Soule after a ten-year marriage that produced a cherished daughter, Barbara. Now he was living alone in room 231 of the Somerset Hotel on Commonwealth Avenue just around the corner from Fenway Park.

Some of his off-time was spent tying fishing flies in his room. On the road, in practically every city except New York, he walked to the park from the team hotel no matter how far it was. "I finally had to stop doing it in Detroit," he said, "because you had to walk through a slum area and you were always getting stopped by winos and bums and gosh knows what kind of people. They didn't know I was Ted Williams, or John Doe, or John D. Rockefeller, or anybody. They just thought anybody who had on a decent pair of slacks had to be a millionaire, and they were always looking to bug you for money or something."

Williams never had liked a lot of people crowding in on him. He always had been an ascetic with regard to smoking and drinking. He even objected violently when he had to sit downwind of anyone smoking cigarette, cigar or pipe.

Now, as the years melted into 1957, his hours away from the field became even quieter. Now he was rooming alone; however, for one five-year period early in his career, his roommate and constant companion was one Broadway Charley Wagner, a blithe spirit and fancy dresser much admired by the punctilious Ted.

"Back around 1941, the year he hit .406, Ted would have a funny sort of a day," Wagner reminisces now. "He'd get up a little before seven o'clock and the first thing he'd do was turn on the radio. There wasn't any TV in those days, of course, and Ted loved the radio.

"Then as soon as he turned on the radio, he'd call down to the bell-captain and have them send up all the newspapers they could get their hands on.

"Ted would read those papers line by line . . . every box score in the American League . . . taking particular note of what the pitchers did . . . how long they lasted in the game . . . whether they were wild or not . . . whether they struck out a lot of people . . . things like that."

Strangest of all, says Wagner, Williams could remember to the final decimal what almost any hitter was hitting and also what any pitcher's earned-run average was.

"After Ted finished the box scores, he'd turn to the theater page. He used to cut out the timetable for all the movies both downtown and in the neighborhoods. Then he'd figure out how many movies he could see before he had to go to the ballpark, and whether he'd want to see another after the game.

"Ted, Lefty Grove and I were always the first ones in the park. Ted was so intense, he used to psyche himself up for games. The better he hit, the moodier he'd get, because that was the way he psyched himself.

"In the room before a game," Wagner went on, "Ted would walk around talking out loud about that day's pitcher and what he was going to do to the guy. 'I'll murder this bird,' he'd say. 'Boom! Right down the middle!' He loved to stand in front of a mirror and make like he was swinging the bat."

Of all his off-field memories of Williams, Wagner marks

41

down as something special one in St. Louis.

"I had come back to the hotel room and found a pile of shavings on my bed. Someone had shipped some new bats to Ted at the hotel, by mistake, instead of sending them to the park where they belonged. It was an off-day, so he started shaving the handles. He always carried a scraper around with him.

"I said, 'Hey, roomie, what the hell you doin'?'"

"Ted said, 'Don't worry, roomie, we're going to win a lot of games with these babies!'

"Just as he said that, he took a vicious swing. His follow-through hit the bedpost of my bed, completely shattered it and the whole damn bed crashed down onto the floor. We had to get the hotel people to send up another one."

Frank Graham, the late and much-loved New York columnist, recalled another "hotel experience" with Williams during his ill-fated World Series in 1946. A friend of Graham's had gone to see Williams in his Hotel Chase room in St. Louis. Williams had had another bad day. The friend knocked, but no one answered. Finally the friend opened the door and saw Williams sitting in the darkened room staring out a window.

The friend left without disturbing Williams. The next day, however, he told Grantland Rice about it. That night Rice called Williams and asked him what he was doing.

"Just sitting here," Williams said in a low voice.

"Well," said Rice, "get up, sucker, we're going out."

Rice and Graham went to Williams' room and the three proceeded to a steakhouse in south St. Louis, careful to avoid the subject of baseball.

Rice asked Williams if he would like a drink.

"Oh, maybe a glass of wine," said Ted.

A little later, Rice and Graham urged him to have another. "Holy Moses!" said Williams, aghast. "You guys are trying to make a winehead out of me!"

But that had been in the 1940's, and this was in 1957, and T. S. Williams was not having even one drink of wine with any newspapermen.

He was just wearing out baseballs.

Someone asked Dominic DiMaggio, Williams' old teammate, if he thought Ted could keep up his pace. Dom nodded. "I know he can," he said. "I remember the first time I ever saw Ted Williams. It was 1938 and we were both in the Pacific Coast League, me with San Francisco and Ted with San Diego. I was sitting beside our manager, Lefty O'Doul, in the dugout watching Ted take batting practice. Lefty took one look at Ted and turned to me and said, 'There's the next Babe Ruth.' And Lefty O'Doul was the greatest hitting teacher I've ever known."

Dom DiMaggio nodded again. "Yeah," he said, "you better believe he can keep it up."

Chapter Four

"Ted Williams is a famous sports figure and therefore he becomes an important news story. But he is merely one more example of psychological dynamism where the hurt, secret or otherwise, brings aggression because of regression."

Prof. Willem Pinard,
Boston University Psychology Department

On April 24, 1957, Williams bombed Washington's Bob Chakales for a game-tying home run—his third of the season and his second in two days. The blow came in the eighth inning, and the Red Sox went on to win, 4-3, on Jackie Jensen's homer in the tenth.

This was curious, in a sense, because Williams might not

have hit the home run if Chakales had not come on in relief of Pedro Ramos. Ramos, the Cuban "palmballer," as he rather euphemistically referred to his slippery pitch (*i.e.*, spitball), was troublesome for Ted because he could tantalize him with slow stuff.

As it so happened, both Ramos and his father had idolized Williams when they were living in Cuba. After Ramos began pitching in the American League, he brought his father to a game. It was the first time Ramos' father had ever seen his son pitch in the United States, and he was also looking forward to seeing his old idol, Williams.

Ramos handled Williams rather well that particular night, and when the game was over, he turned expectantly to his father.

"Boy!" the elder Ramos said, "isn't that Williams great?"

"I would have to say," Pedro remarked sadly, "that that was one of the worst letdowns of my life."

At any rate, things were falling into place for Williams for fair at this point of the 1957 season. He was speeding up rather than slowing down, as had been rather freely predicted as his thirty-ninth birthday approached.

April 25, against Washington, he doubled once and singled twice, and walked in his other three times at bat. Clint Courtney, the Senators' catcher, simply shook his head in the dressing room afterward. "Williams never hits a bad pitch," said Courtney. "He has the most amazing eye in the league."

The rampage in Washington catapulted his average to .455. Williams' teammates, most of them ranging some 200 points lower in the averages, now began predicting he would hit .350 for the year.

Williams had hit safely in eight straight games, his best season-starting performance ever, although he had hit in seven in a row in 1939.

Only Ted refused to get excited. "It's early in the season yet," he said laconically. The years were making him cautious. Once he had said, "The biggest mistake a hitter can make is to not think he is going to hit every time he walks up to that plate. Thinking you're going to hit is the most important part of hitting." But now he seemed reluctant to get optimistic.

The hitting streak stopped the next day, April 26, in Yankee Stadium. The stopping was done by Tom Sturdivant and Tommy Byrne. But Jim Piersall, Williams' needling adversary of the year before, hit a three-run homer in Boston's 6-2 triumph.

Even in that, Williams found a verbal bonus. "Ted has been great to me," said Piersall. "He's been working on me not to get so excited. I think it's helped me."

It is possible that Piersall overrated the salubrious effects of Williams' advice to cool it. Two days later, by which time the Red Sox had split with the Yankees and Ted had gone two-for-six, Piersall and Yankee Bill Skowron almost came to blows on the field.

Now that their "feud" was over, both Williams and Piersall pooh-poohed it and all but denied there ever had been one.

"There was a little feud, all right," recalls Ted Lepcio. "But it never was any big thing. What happened was, one day Williams threw his bat and didn't get fined. A few days later Piersall threw his bat and Mike Higgins fined him. The rest of us started to give Jimmy the needle. He got a little mad—funny, not at us, but at Williams. Like I say, though, it wasn't any big deal as feuds go."

Williams singled as Boston won its fifth straight, 2-1, April 27 in Yankee Stadium. He also singled as the Red Sox were halted, 3-2, the next day.

Then, on April 30, he ran into his old shift-inventing nemesis, Lou Boudreau. "The Frenchman," as Williams called him, now was managing Kansas City. And now, as Ted pointed out, the pitchers were so wary of his ability to hit to left that they were not going nearly so far in stacking the right side of the diamond.

"The queerest thing happened that day," says Williams. "I had gotten to the park early, to work with our hitters. I saw the Kansas City groundskeeper and got to talking with him. We got pretty friendly. I think he was sort of a fan of mine. Anyway, he seemed to like me.

"Finally I thought maybe I could take advantage of the situation. So I said to the groundskeeper, 'You know, fella, that left-hand batter's box you got here, you ought to build it up a little. It's so soft a guy like me can't get dug in there. Too sloshy and soft. What you really ought to do is put some tough clay in there. Then a guy could anchor himself. Your batters, too, of course.' "

Kansas City's groundskeeper was so impressed at this wisdom from his hero that he went right to work on the batter's box.

That night Williams ripped Ned Garver for his fourth homer, a double and single as Boston won, 3-1.

"I think Boudreau found out what the groundskeeper had done," Williams remembers with a grin, "and damn near fired the poor guy. Hell, he was just trying to be helpful."

Not coincidentally, Williams hit .464 for all his games in Kansas City that season, and .526 in night games against the Athletics in Kansas City and Boston.

Until now Ted had been as busy as he wanted to be, which was 100 percent busy on the field and about 10 percent busy off it. For a change he had escaped even the slightest physical infirmity in training camp, and his health was sound through the first two weeks of the 1957 season, surely a surprising if not remarkable achievement for an athlete pressing thirty-nine. It is axiomatic in baseball that any player over thirty is like a thoroughbred horse; neither is ever completely free of some ache or pain.

47

Williams thumped his fifth home run—one of only two Red Sox hits off Tom Morgan—as the Sox lost, 7-5, May 1 in Kansas City. However, when they came home to Fenway to open a series against Detroit on May 2, he began to feel a chest cold.

Manager Higgins took one look at his big man when he turned up at the park. "You're pale as a ghost," said Hig. "You better see the doctor and then go home to bed until you look like a human being again."

It looked like the same old story for Williams. His medical history already qualified for a reading at an American Medical Association meeting.

It had started on July 13, 1939, when he had appendicitis but refused to submit to an immediate operation. Although it is little-known, he compiled his .406 average in 1941 playing on a leg that pained him considerably. He stayed clear of serious injury from then until July 14, 1950, when, at age thirty-one, he broke an elbow crashing into a wall in the All-Star game and was out for two months. He often said that this was the real beginning of his physical problems, and the arm infirmity affected not only his throwing but his hitting as well.

On March 1, 1954, the trouble area moved upward about 12 inches to his collarbone. He was taking part in his first spring workout, fell trying to catch a fly ball and broke his collarbone. A pin was inserted in the shoulder and he missed two months. But on his first day back in the lineup he broke loose for eight-for-nine in a doubleheader against the Detroit Tigers, including two home runs and a double.

June 5, 1954, brought an attack of pneumonia that bedded him for three weeks. Little more than a year later—July 1, 1955—he developed troubles in his back. An arch injury April 18, 1956, kept him on the bench for five weeks.

Such injuries may be part and parcel of baseball, but

48

there was never any satisfactory explanation of Williams' extreme susceptibility to respiratory ills.

The single certainty is that Theodore Samuel Williams was one of history's worst testimonials to clean living. For a man who never smoked or stayed out late and almost never drank and had a passion for sampling almost every new body-building device that came on the market, he was prey to an amazing number of ailments.

His build could have had much to do with it. When he joined the Sox in 1939, he had weighed only 175 pounds. His six-three height gave him the general conformation of a cane-pole.

"There had been a strain of tuberculosis in Ted's family," said Johnny Orlando, the clubhouse man. "And Ted was so skinny in the early days that he thought he surely must have some of the TB in his system. I swear, he worried about it all the time. I finally persuaded him to see a doctor, and the doc had a devil of a time convincing him he didn't have TB. But he finally did convince him."

Something was wrong, though. During Williams' second stint in service, he had what a Marine Corps medic called "walking pneumonia." He was constantly pestered by spring and summer colds after that. As late as 1967, Ted was abed for ten days during the summer with a raging cold. He was not, of course, still playing baseball, but it played hob with his quest for Atlantic salmon on his Miramichi River haunts in Nova Scotia.

"I never could explain it," he says. "All I know is I had colds all the time. It seemed to be a cycle. Once they started, they kept coming back more and more often."

In later seasons, such as 1957, Williams usually kept a king-sized set of vitamins and other nutritional aids handy. So, for May 3 and May 4, he stuffed himself with such nostrums and reflected on past and future in room 231 at the Somerset Hotel.

The Red Sox fans had an opportunity to reflect as well. Over the decades there had been angry enclaves of both writers and left-field-line ticket-holders who insisted that the Red Sox might even be a better team without him. They claimed he often failed to hustle on balls hit to left field (his teammates continued to insist that Williams was the best leftfielder in the game, because of his artfulness in playing the wall in Fenway Park), that he did not trouble to run out all balls hit, and called him the complete individualist.

Some newspapermen were perpetually on his back. Many offered up bones of fact, but they also chewed the bone to the marrow in innumerable cases.

After Ted's Truman-Taft-Marine blast, Joe Williams of the now defunct *New York World-Telegram & Sun* teed off on him. Scripps-Howard's syndicated columnist called Ted "The Cheerless Dragon" and added, "It seems agreed that he has carried his choler to indefensibly offensive lengths."

There will be no attempt here to detail all the published attacks on Williams. Volumes of such material are scattered among Boston libraries and newspaper morgues for those who might be interested. But he did provoke some virulent phraseology from some of the better-known writers throughout the East.

"When it comes to arrogant and ungrateful athletes, this one leads the league," wrote Jack Miley of the *New York Post* as early as 1940.

Austen Lake, one of those who earned Williams' particular scorn, also laid it on. In the *Boston American*, Lake wrote in 1940: "You've sat sullen and aloof in locker rooms and hotels. Often you've looked lazy and careless on fly balls. Occasionally you've snarled things back at the bleacherites. You've taken the attitude, sometimes, that you're bigger than the game."

Yet, in 1952, Lake suddenly turned around and wrote:

There is a limit to this kind of abuse. It's time to give the guy a transfusion of nice, rich, complimentary corpuscles. For the human soda-spigot has his virtues too.

Recently, my telephone tinkled. A pleasantly timbred, feminine voice told me how Williams had spent many hours visiting with her . . . seven-year-old boy . . . when he was approaching a dreaded skull operation.

"You can't imagine the tender sincerity with which Ted talked to the lad," she said. "It was amazing how he could put him on childhood's level, the direct simplicities of which my boy understood and which smoothed away his fears. You know children are quick to detect adult artificiality or a false note, like in a cracked bell.

"Here," said the lady, "was a spiritual therapy beyond medical science. It gave my little one courage to face his ordeal, which restored him to health with a silver plate in his head. Then, later, the lad fell off his tricycle and injured the sensitive skull area and caused a lapse into a silent, morose disinterest which refused to respond to anything his doctor or I could do.

"Once again Ted came to my house and sat for hours with the boy, talking in quiet little homilies—boy language. It wasn't what he said, but how he said it—small things about his own inner problems. It worked wonders and the boy emerged from his despondency and is quite normal now. I credit the cure to Ted.

"In the mind of a boy," the lady concluded, "there is a little of God about Ted."

Columnist Lake went on:

I have had a dozen letters testifying that, often, Williams turns up the radiant sunshine of his grin and becomes a charming person. A hospital head tells me Ted has spent uncounted evenings wandering around the children's ward, squatting on beds, chin-chopping with this or that distressed moppet. And always they say the same thing, that it's astonishing how he has the common denominator of child understanding; that his sincerity is unquestioned; that he leaves the kids saucer-eyed, and warns "no publicity!"

Curious cuss, aintee? How can one reconcile this spiritual side in the most emotional, cuckoo personality in sport—the man we call "Mr. Fidgets" for his refusal to make friends and his surly, anti-social nature with adults. Why does he hide his candlelight of virtue under a sooty coal hod?

He gives away annually thousands of dollars, often to insignificant people including the Red Sox clubhouse steward to whom he endorsed his 1946 World Series bonus check with a gruff, "Here, take this." He is baseball's softest touch and the most noted dinner-tab-grabber and tipper in the business.

Yet he refuses to tip his cap to the hysterical mob, and he won't accept the congratulatory handshakes of his teammates after belting his home runs. Nor will he tarry to felicitate a fellow player after being driven in with a game-winning swat—not till he reaches cover in the players' shed.

Well, I have bopped him for his anti-social boorishness, and may do so again. But the tall whizzeroo reveals a core of moral excellence which should be publicly acknowledged. He ain't as bad as painted! Indeed he may even be a damn sight better guy than some of us detractors.

Yet, the same year (1952), even Arthur Daley, that most temperate of men whose column has been a pillar of *The New York Times,* was driven to observe, "Williams is more hated than liked by those who know him best."

The wolves really came out looking for raw meat in August of 1956 when Williams spit at fans who had booed him for dropping a fly ball. He had been fined $5,000 by Red Sox general manager Joe Cronin. Evidence is that he never paid the fine but the incident drew the bitterest comments of Williams' career.

Arthur Siegel had written in the *Boston Traveler:*

When his own club fines him $5,000, then Ted certainly must be out of line. Ted tested the forbearance of Tom Yawkey and Joe Cronin once too often. . . . That $5,000 fine literally is a checkrein. He now knows he is not baseball's Louis XIV. The French king once arrogantly said, "I am the state." The French king was an absolute monarch to the end of his day. For Williams the domain has ended with a $5,000 fine.

Not only did Williams not pay the fine, but the popular Siegel was altogether premature in predicting the "end" of Ted's "domain." But Siegel had company. "The end is near for Williams," said Milton Gross of the *New York Post,* "but if anything can be said of him with certainty, it is that he still is 'The Kid.' His shameful latest exhibition proves that beyond a doubt."

Of all those, Williams might most emphatically dispute the allegations of Arthur Daley (who, incidentally, was relatively close to Williams), who had said Ted was "more hated than liked by those who know him best."

Williams often said he could not remember playing with anyone he disliked, and that he thought those players
53

would testify to a reciprocal feeling for him. He also was proud to point out that he had never had a serious argument with anyone on the field, and had never engaged in any public ugliness away from it.

The dizzying manifestations of Williams' personality led some to seek out psychologists for an explanation. Professor Willem Pinard, head of Boston University's Psychology Department, took on the job without relish but apparently with some determination.

"It really isn't all that difficult to read Williams' behavior," said the professor. "Each of his actions is normal for his type of person. Such behavior as Williams has displayed is of outwardly being exceedingly independent, yet needing complete approval."

Pinard said Williams was aggressive because he was regressive and that the fans were ambivalent. For anyone less intellectually endowed who might have been listening, he translated:

"Ambivalent" comes from Latin words meaning *to move various ways*. There also is a definition of "ambivalence" as showing both affection for and hostility to the same person. Mob ambivalence [and this clearly was a reference to Ted's hecklers in the left-field bleachers] is displayed by the fans who glory in his perfection, but delight in his little failures. They may be saying, "I worship you and in the process of worshiping you, I hate you." They give Williams their adulation, but they hate him because they are not so famous. Remember, I do not say this about all fans. I'm talking about those who fall into the category of the infantile mob mind.

By his very nature, he cannot accept anything less than complete approval for anything he does. Anything less than complete adulation creates childish reactions. A child always wants to be the center of attention. If it does not get the attention, then the child goes into a tantrum.

Now I have said that he needs complete approval. That includes his own approval of what he does. He seeks perfection because anything less indicates inferiority.

Williams says to himself, "I am the cynosure of all eyes. I am the center of the universe." A mature adult will admit faults in his own makeup. They don't distress him. He feels safe and secure. But Williams regresses, becomes a child again. To cover his regression, he becomes aggressive. Some people withdraw into themselves when they feel hurt. Others get angry. He suffers great anguish. He suffers remorse for his childish angers and deeds. But he isn't likely to reveal the remorse, because that revelation also might indicate inferiority. The infantile personality causes double pain. An apology brings double humiliation.

As for Williams' well-documented generosity and many good works, Professor Pinard responded:

That's perfectly natural for him. He's highly emotional. His friendliness is natural. Everything he does is without premeditation. He may not even know his generosity to the less fortunate, physically and financially, is what we call empathy.

Williams probably overcontributes to charity, overtips. everywhere he goes. That's because his reaction is, "That could be I."

If he's especially considerate of aging people, it's empathy. Some might call it sympathy, but the emotion goes beyond that form. He places himself in the other fellow's plight. Others might withdraw into themselves, but once again Williams is aggressive.

Ted Williams is a famous sports figure and therefore he becomes an important news story. But he is merely one more example of psychological dynamism where the hurt, secret or otherwise, brings aggression because of regression.

Confronted with that lengthy personality analysis in late 1968 at his spacious waterfront home in Islamorada, Florida, Williams frowned downward over his battered T-shirt and faded red walking shorts for a few moments. Even at age fifty, he retained a fearful resentment of intrusions into his private life and, particularly, any attempts to unravel the mysteries of the inner man.

Williams tapped his fingers on the arm of a rattan chair in his living room, glanced out at his private dock and thought it over.

"Yeah," he said finally, "I guess a lot of that is pretty much on the mark. Sure, I overtip. Isn't it natural to see a person who hasn't been as lucky as you are, and perhaps pity them, and try to do a little something extra for them? As far as that regression to childhood goes, I wouldn't doubt it. But it goes deeper than that. It also goes back to a lot of things that happened to me in my career *and especially a lot of things that were written about me.*"

Few would dispute that Williams had some strong points going for him in his treadmillish struggle against a handful of Boston writers. Once he flashed five fingers and said, "That's how many of those guys are ———!" Then he unfolded the same hand perhaps five or six times and said, "And that's how many of them are right guys."

The then baseball Commissioner A. B. (Happy)

56

Chandler agreed with Williams. "Ted's right," said Chandler. "Some of those Boston writers would hit their grandmothers with the bases filled."

"How's that again, Happy?" a listener asked.

"I said," Chandler repeated, *they'd hit their grandmothers with the bases filled.*"

Back in 1950 when Williams had spit and gestured toward a Boston crowd and later apologized, Commissioner Chandler had called him to his office for a friendly chat.

"Ted kept saying about the Boston fans, 'What do they want me to do?' " said Chandler. "He said, 'I hit the ball into the stands for them. I hustle. I make the catches. But they boo me. Or those sportswriters blast me.'

"He's a good boy," said Chandler. "Trouble with Ted is, he's got a persecution complex. He can't understand why people boo him. That's why I called him in. I thought I'd try to help him. When a fellow needs a friend, a fellow needs a friend.

"But," Chandler concluded sadly, "I just couldn't reach him."

That was the story of so very much of Williams' roiling career. But there was also the question of just how many people tried to reach him—to genuinely understand his side.

He was criticized when his first wife gave birth to their daughter, Barbara, on January 28, 1948. Williams was not there at the time. He had been fishing in Florida and had no way of knowing the baby would come five days ahead of time.

Ironically, his second child. John Henry, a boy born in August of 1968, also arrived a week prematurely, while father Ted was away on sporting-goods business.

Little was said of that in the press, primarily because so

few newsmen knew he had not been on hand. As for Williams, once he got the news and hurried to his third wife's bedside in Brattleboro, Vermont, his reaction was typical.

"Look at those reactions!" he said, face crinkling into a broad grin upon sight of the child. "What a set of reflexes!"

Chapter Five

"Here was this guy that knew everything I was thinking. It made me feel downright foolish. I got to believing maybe he was clairvoyant or something."

Dick Donovan

Many of the attitudes so freely expressed toward Ted Williams, both for him and against him, do tend to ignore the most important job he had: hitting a baseball.

By the time he would retire at age forty-two after the 1960 season, Williams would be the lifetime leader of the Red Sox in eleven of their twelve most important offensive departments:

Games—2,292.
Batting average—.344.

Home runs—521.
Slugging percentage—.634.
Runs batted in—1,839.
Runs scored—1,798.
Total bases—4,884.
Hits—2,654.
At bats—7,706.
Doubles—525.
Extra-base hits—1,117.
(Harry Hooper led in triples with 140; Williams had 71.)

In 1957, the Red Sox would not have had a .300 hitter without Williams. The only other outstanding offensive producers were third baseman Frank Malzone, who hit .292 and tied rightfielder Jackie Jensen for the club's runs-batted-in lead with 103; and Jensen, whose average was .281. Catchers Sammy White and Pete Daley hit .214 and .225. First baseman Dick Gernert finished at .237, shortstop Billy Klaus .252 and centerfielder Jim Piersall .262.

Meanwhile, early in May, Williams took it upon himself to try to make it back to Fenway Park just two days after he had first taken sick. Inactivity was wearing upon him. But trainer Jack Fadden packed him right back to the Somerset Hotel for more rest. "You can't play yet," Fadden told Williams.

He was ready to play May 5 in Cleveland. He singled off Stan Pitula in the first inning but his fortune turned to misfortune in the fourth. One of Pitula's fastballs bruised his right forearm so badly that Williams had to leave the game.

X-rays were negative. Doctors gave Williams the go-ahead to resume play two days later when the Red Sox opened a series in Chicago. Comiskey Park was one of

Williams' least favorite arenas in '57. He hit only .237 there that season, the lowest he managed against anyone except for his mysterious average of .214 against Washington back in Fenway. Yet on May 7 his two-run homer off Dick Donovan in the ninth won for the Red Sox, 4-3. He also had a single and three walks.

Williams' relationship with the thirty-year-old slider specialist Donovan was an intriguing one. Donovan had been a twelve-year-old growing up in Quincy, Massachusetts, near Boston, when Williams broke in with the Red Sox and became an instant hero. Although Donovan had fair success against the big man throughout his major-league career, he never could completely overcome his awe of Williams' techniques and his grasp of the hitting art.

"It was sort of an eerie feeling," Donovan says today, "standing out there on the mound and thinking that Williams knows exactly how you are going to pitch him.

"To put it briefly, you have mixed emotions about turning the ball loose."

One afternoon, as Donovan began warming up to face Williams and the remainder of the Red Sox, he spotted Williams chatting with two Chicagoans, catcher Sherman Lollar and outfielder Jim Rivera. Ted was discussing hitting, as usual. Then Donovan heard Williams say, "Just take Donovan over there. He's a perfect example of what I mean."

Donovan looked over inquiringly. Ted invited the likable Irishman into the conversation. "Dick," said Williams, "I am going to tell you exactly how you are going to try to pitch me today."

So saying, Williams then proceeded through Donovan's entire pitching plan for that game.

"I couldn't believe it," says Donovan. "Ted would pick a situation and tell me exactly what I'd try to do. It was amazing. Here was this guy that knew everything I was thinking. It made me feel downright foolish. Maybe he was *clairvoyant* or something."

Donovan always has attributed the fact that the White Sox staff had better-than-average luck against Williams to Chicago's "thinking pitchers." Jim Wilson, Gerry Staley, Billy Pierce and others never tried to overpower Williams. They knew better.

"It was a funny thing about Jim Wilson and Ted," Donovan tells you. "I think Wilson had Ted sort of psyched. Ted would get frustrated and mad at not being able to hit Jim, and Jim would just give Ted a little smile. Jim didn't want to get Ted mad. The smile seemed to say, 'Don't worry, Ted, sooner or later you're going to get to me.'"

Donovan offers some interesting theories about Williams. He believes, for one thing, that there was an unwritten rule among American League pitchers not to throw any knockdown pitches at Williams.

"The reason, I think, was that Ted tried to help everybody in the league, pitchers, hitters, everybody," Donovan says. "He never was stingy with his knowledge. He'd share it with you, and if you couldn't absorb it and utilize it, well, that was your loss.

"Once Ted was gassing with our hitters, and Frank Sullivan, Ted's teammate, came over to him and said, 'Sure, go ahead, you big sonofabitch. Tell those guys everything you know about hitting, so they'll knock my head off the next time I pitch against them.'

"Sullivan was kidding . . . I think . . . but the point I'm making is that Williams was always helpful."

Donovan pointed up an occasion on which Turk Lown had just come to the White Sox from the National League and, presumably, was unaware of this unspoken code that vetoed dusting off Williams.

"Turk had the reputation of being a real hard thrower

and a knockdown guy," says Donovan. "Well, he came into this certain game and 'lowered' Ted. I mean, he really lowered him. This was one of those cases where the hitter goes down, his hat flies off and the ball has gone between the top of his head and his hat. It was that close.

"When the inning was over, Turk came back into our dugout, and you could hear a pin drop. I think if he had said the wrong thing right at that moment, two or three of our guys would have jumped him. Nobody said anything that night, but the next afternoon, in the outfield before the game, a couple of our players went to Lown and told him the score. You might move a hitter like Ted back from the plate, but you don't try to hit him in the head."

For Williams' part, there in early May, he felt that defenses were starting to open up on him in a big way.

"I think they thought I couldn't pull the ball any more," he said. "Listen, I never went up there with the deliberate idea to pull to right field, but I was always waiting for a ball to pull if it came in there just right. Then you're damned right I'd try to pull it.

"But if I had two strikes on me, or a real tough pitcher like Donovan was out there, I'd try to hit the ball through the middle. I may tell you this a thousand times, but it will be true every time: If I pulled, it was on a pitch I knew I could pull, or a ball I was looking for and got. It wasn't usually an accident."

His sense of anticipation against Bob Keegan his next time out in Comiskey Park must have been unusually keen. It hardly seemed fair, one old man mistreating another, for Keegan was only two years younger than Williams, but Ted gave Keegan another distinction to go along with the season's only no-hitter he was to pitch on August 20.

Keegan delivered three home-run pitches to Williams on May 8. The first came in the first inning and went into the upper deck in right field. In the third inning, Williams sliced a home run to the lower stands in left field. That gave him three home runs in his last four times at bat, counting the Donovan job in the ninth inning the night before. It was his fifth consecutive hit and he had been on base eleven straight times.

Williams flied out to left field his next time up, in the sixth inning. But it was dynamite again in the eighth. With Billy Klaus on ahead of him, Williams delivered Keegan's offering into the top tier in right field.

Now he had nine home runs for the season. But all he could talk about was the time he flied out. "I broke one of my own rules and swung at a bad pitch," he said of his futile attempt in the sixth inning. "Actually I swung at two bad pitches before I flied out. I had a 3-and-1 count, then 3-and-2. I could have, and should have, walked."

When it was all over, Minnie Minoso of the White Sox summed it up with a sigh. "Ted makes it so easy to hit a home run," he said. "Like the rest of us bunting."

Williams claimed he never "expected" to hit a home run, but certainly he always "expected" to hit the ball somewhere. The attitude stuck out in every word and gesture. A reporter once asked him how come Billy Klaus had had such a good year in Boston after such a bad previous season on the farm club in Minneapolis.

"Who're you asking, fellow?" Williams snapped.

"I'm asking you," the reporter said.

"Well," said Williams, "that proves how much you know about baseball if you're expecting me to be an expert on a bad year. Old T.S.W., he don't have bad years."

Williams would not homer again for exactly two weeks after that May 8 explosion against Keegan. Characteristically, however, he continued to dwell upon the two bad pitches he had swung at.

"I never even did that back in the old Pacific Coast League days," he said. "Even then, they couldn't get me to swing at any bad pitches. But what they did to me . . . especially in 1936, when I didn't hit a single homer in 42 games in the PCL . . . was get me out on low-breaking curves. Sometimes I'd swing at 'em just as they zoomed down into the dirt. Then some of the fellows on our San Diego team—fellows like Frank Shellenback and Duane Pillette—would talk to me and tell me how they were getting me out. Those guys really helped make me into a good hitter. And you know what?" he sighed. "Those low-breaking curves still give me trouble."

That May 8 would not be the last time in 1957 that Ted Williams would hit three home runs in one game. But it would be the last time for quite a spell. He was riding a .443 average. Of course, it could not go on that way. It never does, even with a Williams. And it did not.

Jim Wilson did the first anti-Williams deed. Thirty-five years old and nearing the end of his big-league pitching days, Wilson kept Williams hitless in four trips in the White Sox park on May 9. It was baseball's hottest pitcher (1.32 earned-run average) against its hottest hitter, and for the day Wilson won.

"He swung at a bad pitch," Wilson said wonderingly. "Imagine that, Ted Williams going for a bad pitch. I've never seen him do that before. Anytime you put the collar on Williams, you've had a lucky day, and you better believe it."

Wilson actually had considerably easier going against Williams than a lot of bigger names. Ted considered Jim a cutie who kept the ball moving enough to be very troublesome.

"Always before," said Williams. "at least once in every game I ever faced him, Jim would give me one fastball and sneak it by me. I never even bothered to look for it, because he wasn't a fastball pitcher, and why worry about a fastball when it's only going to be one pitch out of sixteen or seventeen you're going to get the whole game? So he always gets me on at least one. I know Jim gets a kick out of it, but it does bug me."

Several things bugged Ted for a nine-day period starting with the tizzy Jim Wilson put him in. Two rained-out games in Washington on May 10 and May 11 obviously damaged his timing. This meant he was in action only three days out of the previous nine. Then Washington's Chuck Stobbs and Ted Abernathy hung him up for 0-for-4 and 0-for-3 in the end of the Washington series. The 0-for-11 string dropped him to .403, and when he got all eggs in four times up against Duke Maas in Detroit his average dropped to .382.

Bad Fortnight at Black Rock was not quite over. Williams touched Paul Foytack for a single at Detroit. He doubled off Jim Bunning on May 16 (the night, incidentally, of the storied incident involving Yankees Mantle, Hank Bauer and Billy Martin in New York's Copacabana). The double might have made Williams proud under the circumstances, for he struck out the other three times he faced Bunning.

James Paul Roger Bunning, you understand, was not a bad pitcher. In 1957 he was only twenty-five years old and in his two previous years he had won only eight of fourteen decisions for the Tigers. But '57 was his breakthrough season in a career in which he eventually, on July 21, 1964, was to pitch the first perfect game in the National League in eighty-four years.

That spring Bunning had been viewed as a very "iffy" prospect by his employers. If he were optioned again to the minors, it would be his last time out, and he would be subject to draft by another club. But Bunning had developed a slider in winter ball in Cuba and the Tigers had raised him to $11,500 and he had a fairly sanguine attitude toward the season.

So there was an $11,500 third-year big-leaguer with nothing behind him in the majors but mediocrity, and not a whole lot of that.

Bunning had plenty to prove on May 16, 1957. It was

his first start since he had been knocked out on the second day of the season. He had been called a "six-inning wonder," which no one of Bunning's competitive nature would accept without argument.

Bunning set down Williams on called strikes in the first inning and retired him swinging in the fourth.

In the sixth inning, Williams came up with Piersall on third base and two men out. Under ordinary circumstances Williams would have been walked. Few pitched to him with men on third because of (a) the chance of a run-scoring fly, or (b) with two out, the probability that the merest sort of hit could score a run.

Manager Jack Tighe took a chance. "Pitch to Williams," he told Bunning. On a 2-2 count, Williams fouled off two pitches. Then Bunning came in with a low fastball and the master hitter had struck out for the third time.

Williams doubled his fourth time up against Bunning, in the ninth, and soon scored on a Jensen single. But Malzone's fly-out ended the inning.

Bunning was a 2-1 winner. It was his first complete-game victory in the majors. It is likely he will remember that as long as he remembers his perfect game of seven years later.

"I never thought I'd live long enough to see anybody strike out Ted Williams three times in one game," said Bucky Harris, the former manager then in the Boston front office.

Williams was not quoted on the subject, but it is reasonable to assume that his feelings were similar to those of Harris. From then on it became a matter of vindication for him. "Not revenge," Ted said precisely, so there could be no misunderstanding. "I never hated any pitcher. I mean vindication, for me."

It is possible that he had struck out three times in single games in earlier years. However, the only such occasion Williams could remember was at the very start of his big-league career, against Bobo Newsom, the peripatetic workhorse of eight different teams and seventeen changes of location over twenty-four years in the majors. Newsom had fanned Williams his first three times up in a game when Newsom, then a comparatively tender thirty-four, was pitching for Detroit.

The Bunning thing bugged Williams so much that he took to walking around the clubhouse before games and pantomiming situations in which he would be facing Bunning again. "The score is tied in the ninth inning in Detroit," Ted would drone. "There's a man on and Williams is up. The count is 3-and-2 between Bunning and Williams. There's the pitch. BOOM! There it goes! IT'S OUTTA THERE!"

He had done the same thing, with variations on pitching opponents, in his childhood back in the North Park section of San Diego. But this was the first time he had zeroed in on Bunning as a particular target.

He had plenty to do before getting another crack at Bunning. He was slapped with a $25 fine for throwing his bat into a dugout. And he was left baffled by a total of only two hits in his last 23 times at bat.

The comeback began May 17 in Kansas City. He singled twice in a 4-3 victory over the Athletics to hoist his average back to .379, still 21 points above Mantle.

The next day, a Saturday, Ted doubled twice off blaze-baller Ryne Duren as Boston beat the A's, 7-5. Then on Sunday he was 2-4 against another fireballer, KC's Virgil Trucks.

Came a rainout on May 20, after which Williams singled off burly Early Wynn in Cleveland, and followed that with a perfect day against the Indians.

One of his two hits in as many official times up that May 22 was a homer off Cal McLish that was one of four in the same inning by the Red Sox. Gene Mauch, seldom a power-hitter, started the parade. Williams did his homer bit. Jensen struck out, but Gernert and Malzone delivered consecutive home runs. Now Williams' average had blown up to .404.

Art Houtteman, then in his twelfth year in the American League although only thirty years old, often was a problem for Williams. "His ball was alive and sinking all the time," Ted said. "He pitched me outside and down, and that's a tough pitch for anybody to get hold of."

It did not seem especially hard on May 24 in Baltimore. Williams doubled and singled twice off Houtteman and climbed to a dizzy .414 in the averages.

At this point he had eleven hits in his last sixteen times at bat. "Now even I was beginning to get the idea that I might be able to win the batting championship," says Ted now. "I never felt that way earlier, and I knew it was still far too early in the year to make any projections on how I'd wind up.

"But after all it was getting on toward June, and I was saying to myself, 'You're not doing too bad for an old guy bearing down on thirty-nine, Teddy Ballgame. Maybe, just maybe, you can make it.' "

Billy Loes put the brakes on Ted's five-game hitting streak in the wide-open spaces of Baltimore's Memorial Stadium on May 25. Williams got nothing in two official at-bats against the eccentric right-hander.

However, the halt was quite temporary. Williams next embarked on a nine-game spree. In three of those nine games, he had two hits. Although he hit only two runs in the nine games, off New York's Art Ditmar May 28 and Washington's Pete Ramos on June 2, he was hovering around .440. The shot off Ramos was his twelfth and put him one up on Mantle for the American League lead. This one came in the eighth inning and beat the Senators, 5-3.

He did not go hitless again until June 4 when cutie-pie Billy Pierce, the thirty-year-old left-hander who was embarked upon his second straight twenty-victory season

69

for the White Sox, stopped him in Chicago. But the following night Williams bounced back with a double and single in three times up against his old friend and antagonist Donovan.

"Another thing about Williams up there," Donovan analyzed his favorite subject, "was that he had such great discipline. It was practically impossible to make him chase a bad pitch. And you couldn't fool him. Oh, I don't say it was impossible, but it was damn rare. Personally, I tried to pitch him inside with my slider and away with my fastball. But always, *always*, I tried to keep the pitch down.

"If I had any 'strategy' against Williams, that was it. Number one, never pitch to him with men on base unless you absolutely had to. Number two, pitch him down, hoping for a ground ball or a line single."

Jim Wilson, another of Williams' old adversaries, had another crack at Ted on June 6. Whether by psyching him or just outthinking him, Wilson shut out Williams in three times up.

Williams' mood—already bitter from the New Orleans incident in March and made little less so when he fell into what was, for him, a slump—was not the best that day. The man who "never" argued with umpires got into a rare rhubarb with one of the officials.

After Wilson put across a called strike, Williams turned to plate umpire Art Paparella. "That ball was inside," said Williams.

Paparella shook his head. "No," he said. "It was over the inside corner."

"It was not," Williams persisted. "It was inside." He kicked the dirt in disgust as he strode back to the dugout.

Ordinarily Williams' relations with umpires were perfect. He almost never questioned their judgment and never abused them.

Vinnie Orlando, the clubhouse employee who was Williams' closest confidant besides his brother Johnny

70

Orlando, enjoyed recounting how Williams departed from his volatile personality even in his first year in the American League to use umpires to his advantage:

"Of course the umpires used to skip from one team to another and were always getting a good look at every team. So when Ted got on base, he'd strike up a conversation with the umps. He'd ask them how the pitchers were throwing in, say, New York, where the umpire had just worked a series. That way, Ted would find out from them what the pitchers were throwing to certain hitters, how they were pitching, if they were relying on the fastball or curve, things like that.

"It was beautiful," Orlando smiled. "It was like having a personal scouting system. The umpires didn't mind because Ted never gave them any trouble. But the American League office got wind of it and made them stop."

To the end of his career, Williams insisted that the single worst strike ever called on him was in the 1947 All-Star game in Chicago's Wrigley Field. "It was a low pitch and it was away outside," Williams said. "And I know Jocko Conlan, who called it, never even saw it. I'm not sure why, unless it was that sidearm motion that skinny old Blackwell used to use."

Williams, however, did not remonstrate with Conlan. He walked away without a word.

Conlan wrote some years later in his book, *Jocko*, co-authored by *Sports Illustrated*'s Robert Creamer:

I knew I had made a mistake. The pitch was too low. I should have called it a ball. Here I had called Ted Williams out on strikes in the All-Star game . . . and he didn't say anything.

I've always felt bad about calling that one wrong on Williams, but he never said a word to me about it. All through his career, for all his temperament and his difficulties with the fans and the press, he had the same reputation with umpires that Stan Musial had. . . .

I'd ask American League umpires, "What kind of a guy is this Williams?" To a man, they'd answer, "Jock, he's the greatest."

He never complained. . . .

At any rate, on June 7, 1957, the day after his shutout by Jim Wilson, Ted achieved only zeroes off Lou Burdette in Kansas City. He homered and singled off the Athletics' Gene Host on June 9, but dropped to .380. Alex Kellner and Ryne Duren gave him nothing the next day.

Williams was ready for Cleveland's pitching. In twelve times up in three games, he lashed Dick Tomanek, Don Mossi, Early Wynn and Bob Lemon for six hits. He got his eleventh homer of the season off Tomanek on June 11.

The third game was a beaut.

He tied an American League record June 13 (that he could accomplish such a thing on a "jinx" day was but one more manifestation of Williams' mysterious makeup) by hitting three home runs in one game for the second time that season. As mentioned, he had done it earlier on May 8 against Chicago's Bob Keegan. This day the victims were Wynn and Lemon.

They were "Williams' kind of pitchers," powerful and challenging fastballers. Williams was so irritated with what he considered his poor work in pregame hitting practice that he tossed his bat fifty feet into the air.

Heading toward left field to shag some flies, he stopped beside shortstop Billy Klaus. "Boy, that was lousy, wasn't it?" he said. Except that he did not say "lousy," exactly.

Yet in the next two hours he hit three homers off some of the toughest pitchers in baseball. Two came off Early Wynn and the other off Bob Lemon.

Thus Williams became the third major-leaguer ever to hit three home runs in a single game twice in one season. Not even Babe Ruth was included in that company. Johnny

Mize had done it for the Cardinals in 1938, the Giants in 1948, and Ralph Kiner had done it for the Pirates in 1947.

Williams' first was a three-run shot off Wynn in the first inning. A none-on homer followed in the fifth. None were on, either, when Williams parked another off Lemon in the eighth as the Red Sox won, 9-3.

And it didn't even make the front pages of most sports sections across the country!

That just happened to be the night in Brooklyn when Dodger Don Drysdale low-bridged Milwaukee batter Johnny Logan, Logan charged Drysdale, Drysdale decked Logan, Milwaukee's Eddie Mathews punched Drysdale and a riot ensued. And Williams' feat went to the inside pages.

Chapter Six

"Not only could Ted tell within an inch or so of whether the ball would be a strike . . . but the craziest thing was he could read all my pitches. He made a study of me while we were playing together. So when I went to other clubs, he knew every pitch I was going to throw before I ever threw it."

Maurice (Mickey) McDermott

The first All-Star vote of 1957 was tabulated June 14. Ted Williams was high man for both leagues with 15,255 votes against 14,755 for Mantle. Ironically, Ted now dropped into his worst "slump," sliding to .340 by All-Star-game time.

Inevitably writers began to speculate that Williams was reaching the end of his string. He'd be thirty-nine in just two months, wouldn't he? He was human, wasn't he?

"Williams doesn't have the old snap when he swings now," said a Yankee player who preferred not to be publicly identified. "I know I don't get nervous against him like I used to. I always thought he wasn't human, but I just don't feel that way now. And I think Ted knows he's not the hitter he once was. He takes more pitches than he used to. He doesn't seem to be as sure of himself at the plate."

Williams read that. He read it and wondered. "There they go again," he thought. But in truth he may not have been quite as confident as before.

"Certainly at that age you start wondering how quick you're going to be," he said. "But one thing that always stirred me up and hiked my confidence was that I could always hit Herb Score pretty good, and he was the fastest guy in the league.

"I'd say to myself, 'Hell, I must be able to get the bat around pretty good if I could still hit this guy, at least before he got that awful injury back in May.' "

Vindication Night was coming, too. Vindication against Bunning, who had humiliated him with three strikeouts back on May 16.

Williams loosened up for Vindication Night by doubling twice off Detroit's Paul Foytack on July 11.

Then, before the next game in Detroit, with Bunning coming up, Ted had bet publicist Joe McKenney 25 cents he would homer off Bunning.

He did better than that.

"Bunning always gave me the same trouble as Frank Shea of the Yankees did," Williams said. "He came up and in with his slider, instead of down. I'd see the ball and be looking for that particular kind of slider, and swing all the way from my fanny, and the bat would be—uuugggghhh!—just beneath the ball.

"I made up my mind I was going to get on top of the ball, and that's what I did, and BOOM!"

75

In his first time at the plate, Williams deposited a Bunning slider onto the top of Detroit Stadium.

Next time up, with a runner on, he drove a pitch into the second deck. Writers called it one of the hardest-hit balls they had ever seen.

"The second one was a fastball," Bunning said ruefully. "I thought the fastball was a great pitch—until Ted swung at it."

Still, Williams was at least mildly discouraged, and definitely tired, by the time he reached St. Louis for the All-Star game. It was during batting practice that he turned to an old friend from Florida and said, "Listen, if you think that *I* think that I'm going to match Mantle, forget it. He'll probably play in almost every game. I can't play the doubleheaders, so that's that. . . ."

He had an undistinguished All-Star game July 9 in St. Louis. He was hitless in three attempts. But he was so close to breaking loose that some of the confidence that had been draining off began to eek back in. He hit one ball to first base so hard that it injured Stan Musial's hand. His last time at bat he flied out on a 400-foot drive that Willie Mays had to chase down.

The American League won anyway, 6-5, and Williams departed the thirteenth All-Star game of his career.

Well, he could always remember the All-Star game of sixteen years earlier. And when he did, he remembered it as the most thrilling of his life in baseball.

The 1941 classic was played in Detroit. The National League led, 5-3, as the Americans came up for the bottom of the ninth inning. Frankie Hayes popped out. Ken Keltner singled and so did Joe Gordon. Cecil Travis walked to fill the bases. Joe DiMaggio, big opportunity at hand, hit into a force that sent Keltner across the plate, just beating second baseman Billy Herman's double-play-attempt throw to first base. Now Williams was at bat with two men out, two men on and his team behind, 5-4.

That left it up to Bill McKechnie, the National League manager who seldom was caught short in his cerebral approach to baseball. McKechnie knew that Claude Passeau had struck out Williams in the previous inning, and that Dominic DiMaggio was to follow Williams to the plate, and that Dom could stroke a baseball too. McKechnie thus ordered Passeau to pitch to Williams.

With two balls and one strike, Williams smashed Passeau's next offering into the right-field stands for a 7-5 victory for the American League.

Del Baker, the American League All-Star manager from Detroit, planted a large kiss upon Williams' beaming mug. Art Fletcher, the AL coach from the Yankees, pumped Williams' right hand until Ted had to withdraw it almost in pain. "He really hit the hell out of that ball, didn't he?" Fletcher exulted. "I thought it was going downtown!"

Nothing could ever really top that for Williams on a baseball field. Perhaps, though, he came close in the 1946 All-Star game, if it could be called a game. The American League won 12-0 in Fenway Park in large part because Williams had two home runs, two singles, a walk and five runs batted in.

If the World Series of 1946 was his hang-up, his All-Star history was a somewhat different story. Williams' record for sixteen years (actually eighteen games, including two each in 1959 and 1960) in All-Star games until he retired after the 1960 season is on page 78.

Jim Bunning always emphasized that Williams was "the greatest hitter of my time." It is pertinent to remember that the two hardly met until Williams was in his late thirties. Though the statistic is not handily quoted, one reason Bunning and so many others viewed Williams in that fashion was his ability to reach base in a fashion other than a base hit.

His career total of 2,018 walks was only 38 less than the 2,056 aggregate of Babe Ruth. Had Williams not missed

YEAR	POS.	AB	R	H	2B	3B	HR	RBI	B.A.	FLDG. AVG.
1940	OF	2	0	0	0	0	0	0	.000	1.000
1941	OF	4	1	1	0	0	1	4	.500	.750
1942	OF	4	0	1	0	0	0	0	.250	No chances
1943	(In service)									
1944	(In service)									
1945	(In service)									
1946	OF	4	4	4	0	0	2	5	1.000	.500
1947	OF	4	0	2	1	0	0	0	.500	1.000
1948	PH	0	0	0	0	0	0	0	.000	No chances
1949	OF	2	1	0	0	0	0	0	.000	1.000
1950	OF	4	0	1	0	0	0	1	.250	1.000
1951	OF	3	0	1	0	1	0	0	.250	1.000
1952	(In service)									
1953	(In service)									
1954	OF	2	1	0	0	0	0	0	.000	1.000
1955	OF	3	1	1	0	0	0	0	.333	1.000
1956	OF	4	1	1	0	0	1	2	.250	1.000
1957	OF	3	1	0	0	0	0	0	.000	1.000
1958	OF	2	0	0	0	0	0	0	.000	1.000
*1959	PH-OF	3	0	0	0	0	0	0	.000	No chances
*1960	PH-OF	2	0	0	0	0	0	0	.500	No chances
TOTALS		46	10	14	2	1	4	12	.304	.960

* Two games that year.

all or part of those five seasons (1943-45, '52-'53) in service, he unquestionably would have gone over 2,500 in walks and exceeded the Babe's total by nearly 20 percent.

"You just didn't put anything over the plate for Ted to hit when a game was at stake," said Maurice (Mickey) McDermott, a Williams teammate for four seasons who pitched against him for another five seasons with Washington, New York, Kansas City and Detroit.

"When I was with the Yankees in 1956," McDermott went on, "Casey Stengel had a standing $50 fine for any pitcher who got beat by Williams in a game. That was absolutely inviolable. Casey thought it was stupid to tempt fate, especially when Ted was holding the fate in that bat of his. If you let Ted get a hit to beat you, it cost you $50. So I'll guarantee you, people were careful to pitch around him."

Williams' almost inhuman eyesight (a Navy doctor told him his vision could be matched only by about six men out of 1,000) was invaluable in his intensive and continuous study of those around him, both hitters and pitchers.

Said McDermott, "Not only could Ted tell within an inch or so of whether the ball would be a strike . . . but the craziest thing was that he could read all my pitches. He made a study of me while we were playing together. So when I went to other clubs, he knew every pitch I was going to throw before I threw it."

One night in 1957, McDermott was pitching to Williams' teammate Jackie Jensen. "Ted was in the dugout," McDermott said, "and he would read my pitch and whistle to Jensen. I guess the whistle meant I was going to throw the fastball, because Jensen rifled a line drive back through the middle that missed hitting me in the ribs by about two inches."

McDermott, shaken, shouted to Williams in the dugout, "You big jerk, what are you trying to do, get me killed?"

On another occasion, during his Kansas City tenure,

McDermott was toying with what he called a "two-bit knuckleball." One hit Williams in the back. "And then," McDermott laughed, "it was Ted's time to yell at me. He hollered, 'Hey, bush, you still don't know where the plate is!'

"That's the only time I remember seeing Ted get hit by a pitch, and it wasn't thrown hard enough to bother a snail."

In mid-July of 1957, as usual, it was Williams hitting the pitchers rather than vice versa. He got his 23rd home run July 13 off Detroit's Lou Sleater and his 24th and 25th on July 14 off Cleveland's Bob Lemon and Stan Pitula. He hammered his fifth homer in seven games, and his 26th of the season, off Virgil Trucks in Kansas City on July 16. Trucks threw high and hard but Williams always felt that Trucks was more "straight" than "stuff."

"I'd tell myself, don't swing too hard against Trucks, just be quick, and uuuggghhh! That's the way I'd do it against Trucks. He was a lot like Score in that he threw so hard that when you did get hold of the ball it really flew out of there."

Ted recalled that he had hit one of the hardest balls of his career against Trucks some years before. "He was beating us 1-0 in Fenway, and the wind was blowing a gale in. Trucks had that wind behind him and he was arming the ball right by us. In the ninth inning I was at bat and we had a man on first base and three balls and no strikes on me. Steve O'Neill was managing Detroit then. He went out to the mound and told Trucks he didn't dare walk me, to put the tying run at second base. So Trucks threw me a pitch right in there high and hard and I hit the ball as hard as I ever hit one, and we won, 2-1."

If any number of people had not learned in the previous nineteen years (and that number must have been previously low), the season of 1957 re-established the two verities about Ted Williams: You could not pitch to him, and you could not *not* pitch to him.

"There just isn't any way," said Paul Richards, then managing the Baltimore Orioles. His mind skipped back to a doubleheader the Tigers had played against Williams and the Red Sox in 1946.

"I caught the first game for Detroit," said Richards, "and Williams had got four hits and nailed Pat Mullin to the right-field wall on most of them. Birdie Tebbetts was catching the second game. Fred Hutchinson was pitching. Between games we're in the clubhouse, just gassing around, and Hutch is saying he doesn't care if Williams is the superstar, he's not going to let Ted hit him like he'd hit in the first game. Hutch says he's going to brush Ted back.

"Well, the game starts and Williams comes up. He stomps his feet and digs in and Hutch comes inside with a pitch and Williams leans back a little. Next pitch, Hutch really comes inside and Williams hits the dirt."

Richard's eyes glinted and the corners of his mouth drew back slightly in his tight smile. "You have to get the picture—here are two of the greatest competitors in baseball history, and it's just one man against the other out there now. So Williams gets up and digs in again," Richards went on. "Finally Tebbetts throws the ball back out to Hutch on the mound. The pitch comes in and Williams hits it out of sight. I understand it's the longest homer Williams ever hit.

"Anyway, by the third inning, Hutch is out of the game and back in the clubhouse. I know he's really fuming in there, ready to bite nails, but I can't resist. I sneak back into the clubhouse and leave the door open so I can get out in a hurry. Then I holler to Hutch, 'Yeah, Hutch, you really showed that Williams.'

"Hutch picks up a chair and cuts it loose at me. But I'm out of there just in time for the chair to crash against the door."

The day after pulverizing Trucks' high hard one July 16, 1957, Williams was back at it against Kansas City's Ralph

Terry. This was an entirely different proposition, for Terry was a mix'em-up man (so much so that he was constantly in Dutch with his employers for what they considered overexperimentation) and almost the hypothetical opposite of his rostermate Trucks.

The result was about the same. Williams had three singles and Terry walked him three other times. Then Ted tripled off Tom Morgan in the final game of the stand in Kansas City.

That gave him the most successful trip of his career. Since the All-Star break, he had had 14 hits in 21 times at bat. This topped even his two best records on the road, both of which had come in his banner .406 season of 1941. That year he went 14 for 23 in one road span and 20 for 32 in another out-of-town period.

His homer off Paul LaPalme in Chicago on July 9 was his 27th of the season and his seventh in nine games. Now he was eight points in front of Mantle, .366 to .358.

Williams really had no way of knowing that he was in head-to-head competition with a "new" Mickey Mantle in 1957, a Mantle with renewed confidence in every respect.

Mantle, then twenty-five years old, had been the American League's most valuable player the year before with 52 home runs, 130 runs batted in and a .353 average. In the spring of 1957 he felt he had every point in his favor when it came time to sit down and bargain with the Yankee brass. He had earned $20,000 in 1955 and jumped to $30,000 in 1956. For 1957, Mantle set his mind upon a flat 100 percent increase to $60,000.

In his first meeting of 1957 with Yankee general manager George Weiss, Mantle asked for $65,000. Weiss countered with an offer of $42,500. Mantle quietly demurred and continued to insist upon $65,000.

Weiss went to $50,000, then to $55,000. "And that's final," said the g.m.

"Oh, no," said Mantle, "$60,000—and *that's* final."

Mantle got what he wanted. Although he was hurt off and on during the spring and summer, he played with more élan, and that probably traced back to the secure feeling of having, for once, broken down the front office of the biggest and most successful franchise in baseball history.

Williams meanwhile was little more than a month shy of his thirty-ninth birthday. If his detractors of so many years were not precisely retreating, at least they were not charging with such abandon.

Chapter Seven

"Ted could always kill great fastballers like Score and Trucks and Feller. He was certain that sooner or later they were going to come to him with that fastball. When they gave him the smoke, he was waiting for it."

Joe Coleman

Even Red Sox manager Mike Higgins, the rugged forty-eight-year-old Texan who never was the most communicative of men, was bubbling about Williams in mid-July of 1957.

"Ty Cobb and Tris Speaker and some others could still hit when they were Ted's age," said Iron Mike. "But they didn't hit the top pitchers like Ted does."

There is no use trying to segregate Williams' wrists or

eyes or reflexes or intellect as factors in his hitting in 1957 and throughout his career. They were each integral parts of the whole. If any had been less effective, he would not have been the magnificent hitter he was. But that year a doctor told of a singularly significant episode involving Williams.

Ted had become friendly with a radiologist named Dr. Paul Butler. The doctor also was a fishing buff. He had caught a large salmon on one excursion in northeastern waters, the same territory so favored by Williams, who believes the Atlantic salmon is the finest gamefish alive. Dr. Butler had had a long fight with this particular salmon. Upon his return to his working quarters, he X-rayed the fish to see how many bones had been broken in the struggle.

The doctor had picked out five broken bones. One day, when Williams happened into his office, Dr. Butler displayed the photo and told Ted how to calculate a broken bone in an X-ray photo.

Williams picked up the picture and held it against a bright light. He began tracing bone-cracks. He found not five, but eleven. Then and there the doctor conceded the amazing quality of Williams' eyesight.

But even Williams' vision could not get the bat on the ball every time. He knew this as well as anyone, and, in line with this, he advised pitchers that they would be well-served to watch games on television whenever possible.

"If the pitchers would watch TV baseball," he said, "they'd soon learn the inside pitches are the ones that really do them the most damage. The pitch from the middle of the plate in to the batter is the one that kills the pitchers nine out of ten times.

"I've been saying this all along, but invariably the pitchers will bring up some argument against it. Now I know I'm right. I will guarantee you, nine times out of ten the batter creams the inside pitch."

As for television, Williams explained, "Those cameras

do a great job of showing the relationship between pitcher and hitter. There isn't any argument about where the pitch goes when the camera is zeroed in on it.

"The pitch away from the batter is the safest in the book. Sure, the real good hitter can protect against the outside pitch. But I say, let the good batter do that, if I'm a pitcher. The outside pitch is the one he'll hit for only a single. At most he might get a double on it.

"But you don't see many home runs on outside pitches. I don't care whether it's a fastball or a curve; even the average batter will pull the inside pitch. And chances are he'll pickle it pretty good.

"The good hitters will just plain murder it. That's the reason so many pitchers aren't still around at the end of games these days."

Suddenly Williams caught himself. "Say, what am I giving out this information for? I'm a hitter. Those pitchers should find out things for themselves. I hope they keep pitching me inside forever. They won't, though. They're afraid."

Starting with the July 18 game in Kansas City and continuing through the next five in Boston, Ted went into the most temporary sort of decline. A decline for him, anyway. He had five hits in nineteen trips for a .264 average during this period.

His only hit against Chicago left-hander Paul LaPalme upon the return to Fenway Park was his 27th home run. He had only one hit in the next game against Dick Donovan. But, then, nobody else had any. Williams kept the Red Sox from being "no-hit" with a single to right field.

"It wasn't any cheap hit, either," Donovan conceded. "Jim Rivera was in right field and naturally he was playing Ted deep. Then Ted hit a wicked line drive out there. It was one of his typical sinking shots. Rivera never had a chance to get to the ball. So I couldn't say Ted ruined my no-hitter with a cheap shot. It was about as genuine a hit as I ever gave anybody."

Donovan tried the same system on Williams that others did, with success only in minute degrees:

(A) Never pitch to him with runners on base unless you have to.

(B) Pitch him down, hoping for a ground ball or a single.

(C) Never pitch him high, because that is his power groove. If you make a mistake, it's out of the park. "Downtown," as baseball men say.

Jim Wilson stopped Williams on July 21 without a hit in four times up, ending a ten-game hitting streak. Williams' old nemesis now had allowed him only one single in his last fourteen times at bat against him. But few others handled him that way. He was to have only 24 hitless games in the season of 1957, solid statistical testimony to his consistency.

Kansas City's durable pair of Virgil Trucks and Ralph Terry held Williams to a single in three times up in each of their games on July 23 and 24.

Now Mickey Mantle had regained the batting lead with .362 to Williams' .360.

Anyone who implied or even thought that this was the beginning of the end for the big man didn't know him. By this stage of the season Williams had regained whatever tiny piece of confidence he might have lost because of his advancing age. He believed once again that American League pitchers still looked upon him as the best hitter they had to face. He theorized that, in order to get the best hitter out, the pitchers would have to come in with their best pitch. No one knew better than Williams what each pitcher's best pitch was—he still had that mental book on every one of them—and he simply waited for the best pitch.

"That's why," explained Joe Coleman, a ten-year work-horse for three American League teams but by then out of competition although still a sharp observer, "Ted could always kill great fastballers like Score and Trucks and Feller. He was certain that sooner or later they were going to come to him with that fastball. When they gave him the smoke, he was waiting for it."

Even in one of his rare slumps, Williams refused to change bats and start experimenting like so many other frustrated hitters. Once well into the season, as in late July of 1957, he stuck with a 35-inch, 33-ounce warclub.

Every day he cleaned the bat with alcohol. The first sign of a nick or scratch meant dismissal of that particular bat, which was replaced by another of exactly the same size and consistency.

"He was the first ballplayer I can remember who took real good care of his bats," said clubhouse man Johnny Orlando. "He treated them almost like children. He figured they were a part of him.

"He knew a good bat when he found one, too—no matter where the bat came from. During one of his first spring trainings with us, he had a funny-looking bat, and he was stinging the ball with it. Someone finally asked him where he'd got it. He said he'd picked it up in a store in a little town for a dollar while he was driving through Florida on the way to Sarasota. He wore it out.

"Before Ted, I don't remember anybody using a mixture of olive oil and resin for a better grip."

The story was being told again, during Williams' 1957 drive to become the oldest man ever to win a major-league batting title, of how he had once visited the Louisville bat-making firm of Hillerich & Bradsby, which turned out dozens of Louisville Slugger bats a year to Williams' specifications. On this visit Williams was handed six bats by Bud Hillerich, the company president. He hefted and swung each of them. Then he picked up one and said, "This one's a mite heavy."

Hillerich demurred. "They're precision-made," he said. "They all weigh 33 ounces."

Williams insisted the bats be weighed. All but one weighed 33 ounces. The other was a half-ounce over. That was the one Williams had picked as just a shade off.

Haywood Sullivan, who caught for the Red Sox in the first part of 1957 and went on to become their director of personnel, remembers this characteristic of Williams—the painstaking attention to detail even when he was tired or otherwise off his feet.

One afternoon Sullivan was sitting beside Williams in the dugout. Suddenly Ted nudged the catcher. "What was that last pitch?" he asked Sullivan.

"Gee," said Sullivan, startled. "I don't know. I guess I wasn't paying very close attention."

"Why the hell weren't you?" Williams demanded. "Get in the game! You ought to know what's going on every minute! That last pitch was a slider, knee-high over the outside corner."

"From then on," said Sullivan, "I made damn sure I knew every pitch when Ted was around that dugout."

Chapter Eight

"Ted loved big crowds. When the ballpark was full or near full, you could see he was excited. He liked to put on a show in front of people and you could tell he was 'up' a little more than usual. But I never saw him show any signs of pressure."

Ted Lepcio

The July 23 on which Williams got only one hit off Virgil Trucks was important in two respects.

That was the day Mickey Mantle, Ted's thirteen-years-younger antagonist, played what he then called his "greatest game." Mantle hit for the cycle against the White Sox in Yankee Stadium. He had a single, a double, a triple and a home run that came close to being the first fair ball ever hit out of Yankee Stadium. Thus Mantle closed the hitting gap between himself and Williams to a single point. A day later he seized a two-point lead with .362 to Williams' .360.

For Williams, July 23 marked an embarkation upon a seventeen-game hitting streak in which he was swinging away at an eye-popping .533 average. At the end of the span he had hit safely in 27 out of 28 games.

He finished the series in Kansas City by singling against Tom Gorman in two times up. Then it was back to Boston and a series with Cleveland.

In general, the Indians were not especially good news for Williams. His lifetime Fenway Park average against the Indians was .343, which sounds dandy. However, he hit less (.332) against only one other club (Detroit) in his home stadium. But it was good to be home again, anyway.

He had begun husbanding his strength by resting for much of the playing day. Invariably he arose early and ate a heavy breakfast which varied little from those of his young days—double order of liver and bacon, and a couple of lambchops. He ate little lunch but gorged himself on vitamin pills of all descriptions. "With all the energy I use up on the field and exercising otherwise," he said, "six meals wouldn't be enough for me even if I could eat 'em." At odd times he might eat as often as four times a day, occasionally topping off a meal with a large dish of coffee ice cream.

However, he no longer prowled the moviehouses looking for blood-and-gore and wild-west movies as he had in earlier years when he shared a room with Broadway Charley Wagner. And fishing was just about out during the season, for a change. He spent most of the day in his room, and many days passed when the only others allowed there were a room-service waiter or a valet bringing back a pair of pants or a sport jacket he had sent out to be pressed. He had no laundry problems with dress shirts because he never wore them—only sport shirts with jackets. "Hell, I was thirty years ahead of the times," he was to say in 1968. "I see all these guys wearing turtlenecks, and I was a sport shirt man all my life."

He seldom answered the telephone in his hotel room whether at home or away. Callers were referred to the hotel manager or some other official. The caller was then instructed to leave a number—never a name, just a number. If Williams recognized the number as that of a friend, he might return the call. Or he might not. If he did not recognize the number, the call was forgotten. And the Red Sox club refused to take or pass on any messages to him. His life was completely his own, and the Red Sox and everybody else knew it.

Back in the late 1930's and 1940's, he had spent off-days between theaters and lakes. He and roomie Wagner often went to nearby Lake Sunset and sat in a boat and fished casually, or as casually as Ted was ever able to fish.

Barbara Tyler, who served as Williams' unofficial secretary in affairs involving the Red Sox, remembers his old daytime routines. "He didn't hang around the office as much as some of the others, like Lefty Grove," said the secretary. "My goodness, when I came in in the morning, Lefty would already be there sorting out the mail.

"What I most remember about Ted was how much time he spent fishing during the season. He went out and got a special permit so he could fish in certain reservoirs. Sometimes I'd call his hotel at eight or nine o'clock in the morning, and he'd already be gone."

But this was 1957, and Williams was carefully guarding his energies and his eyesight. One of the standing jokes was that he would not even expend an effort to tip his cap to the crowd after a home run or other outstanding performance because it might take away some of the strength he used for hitting.

Williams' hat-tipping, or lack of it, was a *cause célèbre* in

Boston every season he played there after 1938.

The Red Sox were working their way north in late March and early April of 1939 at the time of the occurrence which presumably kept Williams from ever tipping his cap again. They were playing in Atlanta on April 1—oh, inappropriate day!—and Williams hit a bases-loaded triple early in the game. But he had struck out with two men on base in the eighth inning and slammed his bat to the ground in disgust. In the bottom half of the inning, an Atlanta Cracker lofted a foul into Williams' left-field territory. He had it zeroed in when the wind whipped it out of his reach. Enraged, he picked up the ball and hurled it over the fence and altogether out of Ponce de Leon Park.

The fans let him have it, and, as the story goes, so did manager Joe Cronin, and Williams seldom again offered that tip of the cap with which players from time immemorial have acknowledged applause. He did not even tip it in his very last game in Fenway Park in 1960, although he did doff the lid to a Boston crowd when he returned there as Washington manager in 1969 and was introduced as part of the Red Sox' all-time all-star team.

Cap-tipping was the least of his concerns, anyway, when Cleveland pulled into Boston for a series opening July 25, 1957. Steam all but poured from Williams' bat.

He nailed Don Mossi for two singles in three at-bats the first night. On July 27 he picked on Ray Narleski for his 28th home run, plus a single.

Twice during the 1957 season, Williams hammered three home runs in a single game. But those achievements hardly were any more notable than the ones of Sunday, July 28.

With 22,351 fans raising the roof in Fenway, he pounded Early Wynn for his 29th homer and added a bases-loaded double and two singles. The Red Sox won 9-8 despite two home runs apiece by Vic Wertz and Rocky

Colavito and the desperate defensive machinations of Cleveland manager Kerby Farrell.

Farrell, a relatively imperturbable individual under most conditions, was so unnerved by Williams' attack that he directed Wynn to walk Williams with men ahead of him on first and second base.

This was practically unheard of, particularly since Jackie Jensen, following Williams in the batting order, was having one of his better seasons. But Jensen grounded out to the accompaniment of moans throughout Fenway Park. Thus Farrell's ploy worked although it did not win for Cleveland.

Farrell's reasoning was sound enough. He realized that one of the primary reasons for Williams' hitting in Fenway Park was the visual background.

"I could *see* the ball there," Ted explained. "I could always see it in Fenway better because the background was better and the lights were good, too. I could see it in Detroit and St. Louis and Philadelphia and Cleveland." Especially he liked Washington's Griffith Stadium because it made him feel as though he were hitting "downhill."

But Cleveland manager Farrell had no time to worry about what Williams was doing in other parks. Farrell was still pulling his hair the next evening, July 29, when Williams doubled and singled and scored the tying and tie-breaking runs to zoom his average to .379. This opened up a commanding 27-point gap between Williams and Mantle. More to the point with poor Farrell, Ted was massaging Cleveland pitching at a .532 pace for the year.

This night, Farrell figured what had worked against Williams once might succeed again. In the seventh inning, Tom Brewer singled, Jim Piersall was called out on strikes and Frank Malzone singled to put Red Sox on first and second bases with only one out. Farrell's brainstorm reoccurred. He told Garcia to pass Williams, once again filling the bases.

This one backfired. Jensen rapped a two-run single and the Indians were losers again.

"Fierce, huh?" grinned Williams in an untypical loosening of his conversational downhold.

Fierce it was, and although the Red Sox were some ten games behind the Yankees and hopelessly bogged in third place, the people of Fenway kept whooping it up.

Detroit was next to feel the pinch. Jack Tighe's Tigers might have expected it, with Williams on a ten-for-thirteen rage in his last four games. Bob Porterfield's four-hit shutout of the Tigers got more of a boost from Williams' bat than he actually needed. Jensen's solo homer would have been quite enough, but Williams furnished the remainder of Boston's 4-0 victory with a double and two singles, driving in three runs off Frank Lary.

A Fenway Park crowd of 26,817 watched that one. Although Williams still was getting Bronx cheers and other varieties of abuse from the inimical cluster of fans along the left-field line, he also still reacted to large turnouts.

"Ted loved big crowds," said Ted Lepcio, the Red Sox second baseman. "When the ballpark was full or even near full, you could see he was excited. He liked to put on a show in front of people and you could tell he was 'up' a little more than usual. But I never saw him show any signs of pressure."

The noisy crowd on the evening of July 30 found something extra to shout about. A scorer's decision put them in an uproar.

Harry Byrd had come in in relief of Lary when Williams hit a soft liner behind second base. Shortstop Harvey Kuenn, playing behind second base in the Williams Shift, leaped for the ball. It glanced off his glove. When official scorer Hy Hurwitz announced it as an error, a chorus of boos bounced from the walls of Fenway Park.

Hurwitz began to wonder, himself, and after the game went to Kuenn. The infielder said he had lost the ball in the lights and left his feet too soon, and that it should have been scored as a hit. Even Byrd, the pitcher, agreed it was a hit. There is nothing unusual about a fielder objecting to an error being charged against him, but when a pitcher says a batter got a genuine hit off him, the evidence is overwhelming. Hurwitz thus changed his decision to a hit.

That lifted Williams to .384. But he was still bemoaning his ever-decreasing leg-speed. Even during this streak he often turned to his buddy Lepcio and said, "Teddy, do you realize I'm only five or six hits away from .400? Boy, if I could only run. . . ."

Possibly this was the most remarkable aspect of Williams' altogether remarkable 1957 season. No one knew it better than he did. "He used to use Jim Busby as an example," said Lepcio. "One year Busby got dozens of infield hits for the White Sox because of his great speed, and Ted would just shake his head when we'd remind him of that."

It seems beyond question that Williams would have far exceeded .400 in 1957 if he had had even the speed of an average or slightly below-average outfielder. The fact that he was flirting with that magic figure all season while lumbering rather than running on the basepaths is incredible.

Now he had 29 home runs to go with his .384 average and eight-game hitting streak. As was typical of the whole season, he made up for any brief letdowns by coming back with brutal outbursts.

Bunning, his early-1957 nemesis who had struck him out three times May 16, held Ted to a single in three times up in Boston on July 31. Williams managed only a single in four tries against Duke Maas, Harry Byrd and Frank Lary of the Tigers on August 1, but his hitting string had been extended to ten games.

If there was any great pressure on Williams at this point, it was not apparent. Of course, few people besides Ted would have known of such pressure. He ducked away from reporters after games. When he was not with his buddy Johnny Orlando, the clubhouse man, or alone in his room, one of his few confidants was Fred Corcoran.

The two—the intense and inward-turned Williams and the outgoing and affable Corcoran—had a comfortable relationship both personally and professionally except when Ted was leaning on Fred to go fishing with him. Corcoran hated all outdoor activities except golf (he once caddied for the legended Harry Vardon, and later was a prominent figure in both the women's and men's professional tours). "Ted got me out on the flats once in Florida," Corcoran said in his book, *Unplayable Lies,* "and I wound up with a left index finger that was raw and bleeding and wouldn't straighten out for six weeks. Ted had handed me the rod with an angry bonefish on it. I also got a nice painful sunburn—but no fish."

Corcoran had hooked up with Williams as his business agent in 1946. They never had a contract because neither felt any was needed. Corcoran was the perfect companion for the moody star—a good listener when that was necessary, a compelling raconteur when that was called for. He offered Ted sympathy in his running battle with a group of writers but never quit trying to get him to unbend a little more with them.

Once, said Corcoran, "I took Ted out to visit Bing Crosby, who liked Ted and had told me he thought he understood Ted's problem. Eventually the conversation came around to troubles with the press. 'Let me tell you a story,' Crosby said to Williams. 'I was having a lot of trouble with a guy who had a Hollywood radio gossip column. He was always digging into my private life and printing a lot of innuendoes and half-truths.

" 'One day I ran into this columnist at a golf club and I said, "Hello, Jimmy, how are you?" and he said he was fine. I asked him what he was doing and he was a little nonplussed. He said, "Why, I've got a Sunday night radio show now. . . ."

" 'Well, I said, "That's fine, Jimmy. I'm glad you told me. I'll have to remember to give it a listen next Sunday." And I walked away. He was flabbergasted. . . .' "

Corcoran referred back to that Crosby story. "In his own way," Corcoran said, "Bing was trying to tell Ted that his one chance to end his feud with the baseball writers was to rise above it, to stop batting back every pitch they threw at him.

"The advice wasn't very useful. Bing might be able to react like that, but not Williams, whose idea of a fine game would be to go five-for-five—all over the fence—in an empty park."

Corcoran's analysis differs from Lepcio's; Fred thought Williams disliked playing before big crowds while Lepcio found the opposite true.

Williams was not playing in any empty parks in 1957. Crowds were turning out to watch the ageless wonder all over the American League. His virtuosity enabled the Red Sox to play to 1,181,087 fans in Fenway Park, third highest in the league although the seating capacity was (and still is) only 34,819—a smaller arena than any in the league except for Kansas City (30,611) and Washington (28,669). While their home attendance was third behind New York and Detroit, the Red Sox were the second-best road attraction in the league with 1,186,984 fans. That was topped only by New York and its 1,838,424 road customers.

Chapter Nine

"The finest natural hitter since Shoeless Joe Jackson. . . ."

Arthur Daley

The Red Sox-Chicago game in Boston on August 2 drew 31,007 spectators. Boston's 5-4 victory in ten innings told a great deal about the year Williams was having and its effect on Jackie Jensen directly behind him in the batting order.

Williams drilled his thirtieth homer, a fifth-inning shot off Jim Wilson, and also had a double. The home run was a 420-footer to right field with two men on base and lifted Ted's average to .383. However, it was left to Jensen to provide the winner with a bases-loaded single that made a loser of Bill Fischer in the tenth.

Jensen was known around the Red Sox clubhouse, in the words of one teammate, as "strange." He was not simply opposed to airplane travel; he was terrified by it, so much so that three years later, in 1960, he quit baseball because of it.

"He never talked to me about the flying part," said Williams. "Maybe he figured that because I had been a pilot I wouldn't understand someone being that scared of flying. But I knew he felt that way. When we were making some hard trips—I mean one where we might be up in the air on a 'prop' plane three or four hours—he would take the train or a bus and travel overnight, *overnight, I tell you,* just to keep from getting on an airplane."

Jensen, then thirty and at his powerful physical peak, was uncommunicative in general. But he frequently discussed hitting with Williams. And there was no arguing that hitting behind the master in the batting order made a vast contribution to his effectiveness.

"Jensen never did much in Washington," said a teammate, "and personally I don't think he'd have done any more if he'd stayed there. But he came in and hit behind Ted, and Ted was either getting a hit or getting walked and was always on base in front of Jackie, and Jackie rose to the occasion and got all those runs batted in."

Jensen was the last to disagree. "He straightens out your thinking by taking you back to fundamentals," Jensen put it with characteristic brevity. "He knows what to do and he knows how to tell you what to do, in terms you can understand. He's a great teacher of hitting as well as a great hitter."

Jensen was not the only one Williams was helping. He had advised Jim Piersall: "If you're afraid when you get up to that plate, you might as well just quit baseball. You might as well be selling insurance or working in a bank or something. You can't hit if you have the slightest fear. But why be afraid anyway? What the hell can they do to you?"

The latter question conveniently overlooked the fact that there is a great deal a pitcher can do to a hitter in the way of physical damage if he so desires. Just because pitchers shrank from dusting off big Ted did not mean they took the same attitude toward less gifted batsmen.

However, Piersall reacted to Williams' advice. "Boy, he loves to teach the game," said Piersall. And even though Piersall hit 32 points less in 1957 than his previous year's average of .293, he might have done far worse had it not been for Williams.

Ted's own power production dropped off slightly in early August. There was to be a spell of ten games between his 30th and 31st home runs. But he was making contact regularly, which was what counted.

He singled twice off Billy Pierce, August 3, in an 8-7 victory over the White Sox. He followed that with three singles in four times up against his old pal Dick Donovan, August 4. At that point he had five singles in his last eight times at bat and was sitting on a .389 average for a nineteen-point cushion over Mantle.

August 6, 1957, must have brought a curious admixture of feelings in Williams. He singled once in three times at bat against Ray Moore as the Red Sox lost to Baltimore, 2-1, in the opener of a road trip. That was the day that Lou Boudreau, the man who started the shift that caused Williams so many problems, was fired as manager of the Kansas City Athletics.

Wrote Arthur Daley of the *New York Times*:

> Boudreau departed at about the same time that ballclubs began abandoning the full use of the "Boudreau Shift." . . .
> By cagily punching an occasional shot to left, Ted

automatically has made the defenses so honest that they don't dare gang up on him the way they once did. Thus does the Williams batting average remain at inordinately high levels. . . .

Mickey Mantle is twenty-five years old. That's why Ted's gallant bid for top honors must evoke admiration. It demonstrates with searing clarity the true greatness of Theodore Samuel Williams.

Who else is in his class? There is only one—Tyrus Raymond Cobb. . . .

As a thirty-eight-year-old, Cobb batted .378. As a thirty-eight-year old, Williams batted .377. At that same age, Rogers Hornsby had an average of .338 (which still is extraordinary); Tris Speaker hit .304, and Babe Ruth hit .288.

The finest natural hitter since Shoeless Joe Jackson, Williams still is a delight to watch in action. . . .

A delight to Arthur Daley and millions of fans, surely. To opposing pitchers, hardly.

He raked Baltimore's Connie Johnson for a double and single in five times up in Baltimore on August 7. He added insult to injury with a most un-Williamslike act in the eleventh inning. His single took off on a line to deep right-center. Jim Busby, the Orioles' centerfielder so admired by Williams for his speed, fumbled the ball on the pickup for an error. Thus Williams moved on down to second base.

Mickey Vernon, up next, dribbled a slow grounder to the right of first baseman Bob Boyd. Again it was a bobble. When Boyd finally found the handle, his hurried throw to Johnson covering first base was low, and Johnson had to stretch to catch the ball.

First base umpire Eddie Hurley flashed the "out!" sign. Almost immediately he shifted into the hands-flat-and-down "safe!" position when he saw that Johnson's foot had come off the bag.

The irate Johnson began arguing with Hurley while Johnson was still sitting on the ground.

Williams wasn't sitting. Williams was running. He plodded past third and on over the plate while Johnson was continuing to argue with Hurley. The Red Sox eventually scored another run and won, 5-3.

"Unusual for me," said Ted. That was fine understatement. He attempted to steal only a single base in all of the 1957 season, and was thrown out.

This sliding business became an "item" with Williams that season—not because he slid often, but because he did not. Frank Frisch, the old Fordham Flash and big-league manager, used this as part of a rap against Williams.

Frisch was addressing the Bowdoin College Club of Boston late that season. In passing he picked his all-time outfield: "Tris Speaker, Ty Cobb and Babe Ruth." Inevitably came a voice from the audience questioning the absence of Williams on any all-time selection.

"Williams would come later, maybe, in the era of the 1940's," said Frisch, trying to kiss it off. But when the crowd persisted, Frisch let it all out.

"I like aggressive fellows," he said. "When you play ball, you ought to play it all the way. You don't want a caddy."

This was an obvious reference to Williams' frequent removal late in games in favor of Gene Stephens, an excellent defensive man.

"Is Williams a great defensive player?" Frisch demanded of his audience.

There were shouts of "Yes!"

"Is he . . . has he been an outfielder who charged a ball and threw somebody out?" Frisch went on. "Sure, Williams is a good hitter. A terrific hitter. But I don't want

to see him play. I'll be frank about it. I want aggressiv
outfielders."

He paused, then asked: "Can Williams run?"

One of his listeners retorted, "How about the time he
slid into second base?"

Frisch looked incredulous. "You mean to say Williams
actually *slid?*"

Along with his power output, Ted's RBI total also wa
stationary from August 3 through August 13. But his two
singles off Baltimore's Billy O'Dell boosted his average to
.390 on August 8. Two more singles August 9 off Pete
Ramos brought his hitting streak to seventeen games.
During that seventeen-game streak he had batted .533.

He walked the first two times up against Washington's
"submariner," Ted Abernathy, the next night. He
grounded out in his last two attempts.

His longest streak of the year was ended.

Chapter Ten

". . . The word around the league was that Ted was slipping a little . . . starting to check his swing. He never did this before. Well, the next time I pitched against him I was looking for him to ease up on the swing. I threw him a high knuckleball and he hit it into the bleachers. That was the last time I listened to that kind of talk."

Ned Garver

Manifestly the most important factor in Williams' inability to drive in runs during this span was the reluctance of pitchers to give him anything to hit with men on base. This was underscored August 11 in Washington when he entered the second game of a doubleheader as a pinchhitter and was intentionally walked by Truman Clevenger.

That walk blotted out the all-time major-league record for intentional passes in one season. It was Williams' 27th in 1957 and brought down Duke Snider's high of 26 set just the year before in the National League.

Obviously the Red Sox were not going anywhere in the American League race. They were still third and twelve games behind with only 44 games still to play. The Yankees were in front by 5-1/2 games over the second-place Chicago White Sox. But the entrance of Casey Stengel's bristling Yanks into Boston furnished one of the year's conversation pieces.

Now it was Williams head-to-head against Mantle. Ted led his junior rival by eight points, .387 to .379, in the averages. Mickey had 32 home runs to Ted's 30.

In the week just prior, Mantle had hit a blistering .520 and picked up 11 points to .379 while Williams had faltered two points down to .387. Williams was hitting .343 against the Yankees while Mantle was going at a .310 clip against the Red Sox.

After 110 games, Williams' averages against each club in the American League read like this:

TEAM	AT BAT	HITS	AVERAGE
Cleveland	47	25	.532
Kansas City	57	23	.404
Baltimore	57	21	.368
Chicago	55	20	.364
Detroit	56	20	.357
New York	35	12	.343
Washington	44	13	.295

Thus, although Williams was hitting 33 points higher against Mantle's first-place club than Mantle was hitting against Williams' third-place team, Ted still had his second-worst average for the year against the Yankees.

Old Fenway bulged with its biggest crowd of the season to date that Tuesday night, and its habitués both old and young groaned in unison.

The coupling of Williams and Mantle had its ironies. Not only were they the two most intimidating hitters of the era, for power (Mantle) and for both power and average (Williams), but they were complete opposites in many respects.

Item: Williams' personal brashness was the antithesis of Mantle's rural-oriented diffidence and shyness.

Item: While Williams had a hard time running around the bases much faster than the average thirty-eight-year-old man in the stands could have, Mantle had blinding speed when he was not limping from one of his many injuries.

Item: They would pick the same month, February of 1969, for striking decisions in their careers. That was the month Mantle quit playing for the Yankees "because I can't hit anymore, I can't steal anymore, I can't go from first to third on a single anymore." And that was the month Williams bent to the pleas of Washington Senators owner Robert Short and became a manager after vowing for decades that he never wanted any part of that sort of thing.

Mantle's Yankees won that game in Boston. Mantle exploded a 400-foot, two-run homer to right in the seventh inning and added two singles for a perfect evening in a 3-2 victory.

Williams singled once in two official appearances. He also was intentionally walked once by Tom Sturdivant (raising his record total to 28 for the year) and waited out the young right-hander for another walk.

This, too, was typical of an oppositeness between Ted and Mickey. Mantle's strikeouts were appallingly frequent. Williams was difficult to strike out. He averaged only about 30 percent as many strikeouts as Mantle.

But Mantle that night crept within four points of Williams with his .384 to the leader's .388.

The news was better Wednesday afternoon, August 14. In the second inning, Williams leaned into an 0-1 delivery from Don Larsen and rocketed it into the left-field screen above the 37-foot wall. Two men were ahead of him and a new season-record crowd—this one of 36,207—shook the park as he trotted in with homer No. 31. Ted also singled to go 2-for-3 while Mantle was 1-for-4. Now the pendulum was swinging back Williams' way, .390 to .382, although he remained two home runs behind Mantle.

Ted's all-around rampage had started even earlier. In the first inning, Yankee lead-off batter Hank Bauer sliced a ball off the left-field wall. Hoping to capitalize upon Williams' aging legs and arms, Bauer made for second. But Ted played the ball on the bounce, fired a perfect throw to Gene Mauch and retired Bauer at second base.

That was about the time an exuberant Boston customer broke out a huge banner: "TED WILLIAMS—GREATEST AMERICAN SINCE GEORGE WASHINGTON!"

Boston lost the series' rubber game Thursday but the management benefited to the tune of another crowd of 30,004, bringing the total for three games to 101,858 fans. And even New York's 6-3 triumph could not prevent Williams from gaining on challenger Mantle. Ted singled and doubled off the left-centerfield fence, spelling the end of Yankee pitcher Bob Turley's day and increasing his average three points to .393. Mickey struck out twice and walked three times to drop back two points to .380.

Williams had enjoyed the series with the Yankees for more reasons than his batting average. New York catcher Yogi Berra was one of his personal favorites, and Williams got a special charge out of going to the plate when Berra was behind it.

Ted's favorite story about Yogi involved an incident

108

some years before. "Johnny Pesky was at bat, with me on deck," he recalled. "Pesky popped up a little foul that really wasn't high enough for one man to call for it. Dick Kryhoski was playing first base for the Yankees. He and Yogi came together head-on, I mean SMASH! Both of them went down. Somehow the ball stuck in the webbing of Kryhoski's glove, but he was out cold, completely unconscious. Why, I'd seen dead Atlantic salmon that showed more life than Kryhoski did lying there on the ground.

"Meanwhile, as they tried to revive Kryhoski, Yogi was wandering around in a semi-daze. Finally somebody got Kryhoski up and on his feet. He went back to first base and the crowd gave him a tremendous cheer.

"Anyway, Yogi is putting his mask back on and I'm stepping into the box. Yogi rolls his eyes at me and says, 'I got a pretty good *collusion,* too, and *he* gets all the cheers!'

"I was laughing so hard I made the third out."

A stiff neck put Williams on the bench for the August 16 game in Washington. The neck resulted from the colds that were constantly plaguing him. Manager Higgins knew it. There was seldom any friction between Williams and Higgins (or Cronin or McCarthy or O'Neill or Boudreau, for that matter) over whether he would or would not play. They all knew he would play if he was physically able. "We have a perfect understanding, Ted and I," said Higgins. "If he's up to snuff, good. If not, he doesn't have to play. Nobody knows more about Williams' body than Williams. Hell, he's practically a scientist about it."

Even when he was too sore or too sick to play, Ted kept swinging the bat. He practiced nighttimes in his hotel room with a 50-ounce model. The style never changed whether it was in a room or a ballpark.

Invariably he took a stance leaving ten inches between the tips of his toes and the plate, or an imaginary plate. His feet were spread 33 inches apart. His stride into the ball was ten inches. No more and no less.

"He had one of the shortest strides ever known to man," said the admiring Mantle. "But, by golly, it never seemed to cut down on his power."

Williams' bat was just about parallel to the ground, and his follow-through spun him completely around.

The eight-game spread between August 17 and August 25 was not good for him. He had only five hits, of which the only extra-base knock was a double, in 27 times at bat. His average slithered down to .378 while Mantle was hanging in at .376.

Ironically, on August 18, Williams received the Hickok Award as the outstanding athlete for the month of July. "I won't deny it feels sort of odd to be getting an award right while you're in a sort of slump," he admitted.

In fact, Williams batted in only one run between August 14 and September 17. "What happens," said Ned Garver, Kansas City's thinking pitcher, "is that the men aren't getting on base in front of him. So pitchers are pitching more to him and not walking him as much. If they had men on base, they'd walk him more because he can really hurt you with runners on. But the hitter never lived who could knock in a run with nobody on base, unless he hit a home run.

"My theory on Ted always has been that when he can hurt you, forget it! Give him a walk."

A small smile spread across Garver's choir-boy face. "A few weeks back," he said, "the word around the league was that Ted was slipping a little. You know, starting to check his swing. He never did this before. Well, the next time I pitched against him I was looking for him to ease up on the swing. I threw him a high knuckleball and he hit it into the bleachers. That was the last time I listened to that kind of talk."

Williams always after was delighted with Garver's story, but at the time he was complaining about some sore feet.

"Why shouldn't I have sore feet?" he asked. "I'm on 'em all the time. I'm on base more than anybody else in the game, and if you don't believe it, just check the records.

"If I'm not hitting, I'm walking. Naturally a guy who hits .240 gets more rest during a game, and I'm not saying that to belittle any .240 hitters. It just stands to reason."

Williams also kidded his catchers about that. "Every day I walk or run 320 feet out to where I stand in left field. Then I walk or run 320 feet back again. That's roughly nine times a game. Nine times 640 feet is 5,760 feet. So I use up more than a mile a game just going to my position. All you catchers got to do is walk from the bench to the plate."

Sometimes, he said, he thought he'd like to skip a game. "But if you start doing that," he mused, as if to himself, "you find it easier to miss another. And then another, and another, and pretty soon you're acting like an invalid. And then you're not even playing 75 games, and you're being paid to play a lot more than that, and besides it isn't any fun playing just 75 games.

"Beyond that, once a game starts, more often than not you get into it and forget all about how tired you are or about how you originally didn't feel like playing that game."

In Kansas City, August 26, the king of the hitters broke the ice with a pair of singles off Ralph Terry. He came back the next night in Detroit with a home run off Paul Foytack, his 32nd of 1957 and the 450th of 521 he was to hit in his career.

Now he was making no bones about it: He not only wanted the batting title—he thought, perhaps for the first time that year, that he had at least an even chance of winning it for the fifth time. "I want this batting championship so bad I can taste it," he said.

He also was beginning to pull the ball to right field more often. "It's about like always," he said. "Over the last half

111

of the year, you hardly ever saw me hit to left field."

Fans were rallying more than ever to Williams' side in his twin duel with pitchers and age. Letters poured in from the crippled children to whom Williams had contributed so much with his support of the Jimmy Fund (of which he talked so little, as if he wanted to shield his benevolence from any public view).

One man wrote a letter to a Boston newspaper. The letter said: "Ted Williams is not a team man. He plays solely for the glory of Mr. Williams. Want to blast me for that? My telephone number is WA3-9881. (Signed) Al Brown."

The letter-writer later said he received more than 150 telephone calls, and at least 85 percent of those were critical of him and in support of Williams. "Most of the time," Mr. Brown said plaintively, "the people calling were so mad I never ever got to answer them back."

Most of Williams' critics remained either in the press box or down the left-field line. But he also had some feverish adherents among newspapermen. "Knights of the Keyboard," he called them, but there were many he genuinely liked and who reciprocated the feeling.

Jimmy Cannon, the syndicated columnist out of New York, presented a mixture of praise and censure:

In left field, his stance always was one of indifference. It was as though he were leaning against an invisible fence. There was never that tension that tightens the bodies of other outfielders, that clenched posture which indicates the anticipation of excitement. The pursuit of a baseball couldn't have moved Williams much although he did smash himself up going into a wall for a fly ball in an All-Star game (1950).

The defensive part of the game has to bore him. That was what delayed him coming to bat. He was an average fielder, but not as awkward as a lot of biased reporters contend. He was the only .400 hitter who didn't run fast.

Never did Williams seem to be one of nine. He was a man imprisoned in his own identity, which he refused to share with the others in the common cause of the team. But when he was the hitter he was Ted Williams, not one of the Red Sox. Then he was separated from his unwanted accomplices, his talent a private possession, poised and oddly gentle.

The conspiracy was clear to him then. The nine players on the other team were all against him. He was a suspicious man. It was as though he wished the unpopularity on himself.

As a fielder, Williams became part of the majority arrayed against a hitter. Any one of his side could defeat the batter. It was an accident when the ball was hit to him. He couldn't control the direction of the fly, or the grounder.

Williams' 33rd home run came off Bunning—more sweet revenge for that three-strikeout ignominy of May 16—in Detroit on August 28. But Duke Maas shut him off in one time up the next night and his average dipped to .379.

He had hopes for a big night August 30. After all, he was turning thirty-nine, and very few baseball players are able to celebrate their thirty-ninth birthdays with a .379 average. Williams, in fact, seldom celebrated a birthday in any fashion.

One of the exceptions had been birthday No. 36. Three dozen of his closest friends—no active baseball players and only two sportswriters—had whipped up the gathering at Jimmy O'Keefe's Restaurant across from Fenway Park.

Participants included Johnny Buckley, a theater manager who had become friends with Ted through his mania for movies; Captain John Blake, adjutant of the state police who had met Williams by handing him a speeding ticket; and other old friends, bellhops, doctors, druggists, and so on.

Williams passed out cigarette lighters emblazoned with Red Sox emblems, the name of the recipient and his own signature. When a six-year-old boy got up and sang, "She's My Mom," Williams was the first to applaud. "That was wonderful," he said. A chef brought in a huge cake, which called for a rendition of "Happy Birthday, Dear Teddy."

"Dear Teddy" had himself a glass of ginger ale while most of the guests (the six-year-old excluded) were socking away the booze as fast as it could be carted in.

His thirty-ninth birthday was not so joyful. There was no party; the Sox were playing in Baltimore. And Ted managed only an infield single in his last of five times up. That sheared his lead over Mantle to a mere .0004. That day Mantle had hammered his 34th homer and gone 3-for-4 altogether against Washington, moving up to .3764 against Williams' .3768.

Williams lost the batting lead to Mantle—.378 to .377—August 31 in Baltimore when he had a single in three times up.

Then that old devil that was forever tracking him—the common cold—came back again. Williams fell sick at almost the same time Mantle was sidelined with shin splints.

"Looking back on it," said Dr. Ralph McCarthy, the Red Sox physician, "we can see that Ted has had a chest cold for three weeks. Now we think the best thing to do is give him complete rest and get the thing cleared up. Ted's been bothered by this upper respiratory condition ever since he came back from Korea. Evidently it comes back every year either in the spring or fall."

Just about then, a Boston newspaperman said he had seen a medical report that showed that Williams had a chronic lung condition. That wasn't any sensational news in itself, since various doctors had speculated in the same

114

vein for years, but the writers also predicted that Williams probably was through as a baseball player because of it.

Williams was enraged. "I'll get back out there if I have to go in on a stretcher," he said.

He did not play in a game from September 2 through September 16. He went back to the Somerset Hotel and rested and stoked himself with vitamin pills and prescriptions and some potions of his own choosing, and browsed through his baseball and fishing literature, and tied a few fishing flies.

"Isn't it funny?" he asked himself, thinking of the persistently pesky colds. But it wasn't funny where they had apparently started, back in Korea.

Doubtless he gave considerable thought during those two weeks to his service periods. Both had been surrounded by peculiar circumstances.

He started his big-league career with four spectacular seasons in Boston—.327 with 31 home runs and 145 runs batted in in 1939, .344 with 23 home runs and 113 RBI in 1940, the stupendous .406 average with 37 homers and 120 RBI in 1941 and .356 with 36 home runs and 137 RBI in 1942. In 1941 he had won the All-Star game for the American League with a ninth-inning homer. His 145 runs batted in and 107 walks in 1939 were records for a rookie. In both 1939 and 1942, he had led the American League in total bases with 344 and 338.

Of those early thrills, easily the biggest was his All-Star swat. Williams had come to bat in Detroit with the Americans trailing the Nationals 5-4 in the ninth. Two men were out, Joe Gordon on third, Joe DiMaggio on first. Williams accepted two balls and one strike from pitcher Claude Passeau and then unloaded a home run into the top tier of the right-field pavilion for a 7-5 victory.

But in 1942 Williams was placed in the 1-A category by his Selective Service Board. He asked for a deferment on the grounds that he was supporting a family, and was reassigned to 3-A virtually on the eve of his induction. On March 10, 1942, he had walked into the Red Sox clubhouse in Sarasota and explained his position in a long session with newsmen.

Criticism rained down on him from fathers and mothers of servicemen. Then, as Harold Kaese put it in the *Boston Globe*, "aware of his precarious position before the American public but convinced of the righteousness of his deferment," Williams said flatly he was going to play out the 1942 season as best he could.

"If I didn't think I was right and deserving, and if it were not so important to my mother that I play baseball, I wouldn't even attempt to face this thing, this unfair criticism," he said.

"I never have promised anybody I would enlist at the end of the season, but I'm thinking of enlisting in the Navy, and that's where I'll probably go."

He spoke of his financial situation, which was not the best. "Last year I took out three annuities. If I play this year, I can pay them all up. If I don't pay them, they lapse. They're only for $5,000 or $6,000 but that's a lot of money to me.

"President Harridge of the American League called me the other day. He told me to keep my chin up, that I was right or I wouldn't have been deferred, and told me to conduct myself as I did last year."

Williams, making quite a lucid case for a twenty-three year-old, said Red Sox president Tom Yawkey, manager Joe Cronin and general manager Eddie Collins had urged him to enlist.

That fall, after his league-leading .356 season, he did enlist in the Navy. He transferred to the Marine air arm, served as an instructor at Pensacola, and on May 8, 1944, married Doris Soule. The marriage lasted eleven years almost to the day, after which Williams turned over to his former wife a lump sum of $50,000, alimony of $6,000, and, he added emphatically, "a $55,000 home."

It was during Williams' stay as an aviation instructor at Pensacola—but before his marriage to Miss Soule—that he had given one of his rare explanations of his frequent imbroglios with the Boston press. Huck Finnegan of the *Boston American* was visiting with Williams at the home of Lt. and Mrs. Forrest Twogood at Pensacola, and Williams was detailing, for Mrs. Twogood's enlightenment, his war with the Boston news media.

"First," said Ted, "let's take the Most Valuable Player award. My first year (1939) in the league, I bat .327 and lead in runs batted in with 145. Joe DiMaggio hits .381 and the Yankees win the pennant. Okay, honestly I don't deserve to get the MVP thing.

"Second year, I bat .344. I hit No. 3 most of the time, which means I can't repeat as RBI leader. That's Hank Greenberg's great year. He leads the league in RBI with 150, in homers with 41, and bats Detroit to the pennant with a .340 average. Okay, again, I don't deserve the MVP. But I've been hitting pretty good all the same.

"Third year, I bat .400 all year long. Everybody's trying to stop me, and they can't. I wind up at .406, first time anybody since 1923 has hit above .400 in the American League, and there's been a lively ball around for twenty years. The Red Sox go from fourth place to second place, and don't you think Williams is at least partly responsible?"

He answered his own question. "I lead the league that year, 1941, in runs scored (135) and home runs (37) in addition to hitting .406. But I don't get the MVP. DiMaggio hits in 56 straight games, but bats 49 points lower than I do, and he's MVP.

"Understand, now . . . it's the writers that are doing the voting, not the managers.

"Okay, take my last year—'42. I lead the league in batting again (.356) and in RBI (137) and in home runs,

117

but I don't even get a smell of the MVP because the writers say I loafed in a couple of games.

"Loaf? We had second place clinched when I started to 'coast.' I couldn't go up, couldn't go down. I wasn't hurting the team, only myself. And I had plenty on my mind. I had enlisted and was trying to straighten out my financial tangles.

"It's the same way about my domestic life. One writer says, 'What can you expect of a fellow who doesn't go home to see his mother in the winter?' But let's not go into that again.

"Now take this 'girl situation.' Every time I go up to the plate in batting practice, some guy I never saw before comes up to me and says, 'I'm from such-and-such a paper or news service. My managing editor sent me out here to get a story on you and your girlfriend.'

"So I really get steamed. I say, 'Well, I'm not looking for any story about your managing editor and his girlfriend, so SCRAM!"

"They all get on me, and I'm never the Most Valuable Player, because I don't want writers butting into my personal affairs? Why can't they stick to baseball? They're baseball writers, aren't they?"

On that occasion, Mrs. Twogood asked Ted if he had given much thought to the subject of marriage. Williams replied that he did not want to get tied down.

"Dough's all that counts," he said. "Who's going to take care of me when I can't swing a bat? It doesn't take them long to forget you. I'm in a business that's a 'career against time!'

"A big-leaguer's got about ten years to pile it up. If he doesn't, nobody's going to come around knocking on his door and kick in to him when he's through.

"I'm not reaching for the moon. But I've come down from $250 a day to $2.50 a day, and that's a sharp drop.

I've already lost one year of baseball. I might lose three more.

"Besides, how do I know I'll be any good when I get back?

"I don't want much. Just enough to open a sporting-goods store so I can have plenty of guns and fishing rods around me. And I want enough time to myself so that I'll be able to do all the hunting and fishing I please."

It was during this first stretch of military service that Williams acquired a taste for Florida fishing that he never lost.

"A buddy and I scrounged up ration tickets for enough gas to get us just about to Everglades City, which is down the west coast from Pensacola and a few miles east of Naples.

"We caught a lot of snook the first day and threw 'em back. Since we weren't going to eat them, I couldn't see any sense in keeping them, and I've felt the same way ever since.

"But that night we were visiting a fishery and a man told us he was paying 11 cents a pound for snook. So we went back the next day and caught 110 pounds of snook and sold 'em to the fishery for $12.10.

"That's the only time I ever sold a fish."

It was the last time he had to. He was discharged in late 1945 and came back to Boston vowing no more feuds with fans or writers. Oh, sweet irony.

Then it was all baseball again from 1946 until 1952 when, on February 7, the Marine Corps recalled Ted to active duty for two years.

If Williams had thought his earlier Marine tour had had its bad moments, he found out what it was really like in 1952 in Korea. There he was a member of Pantherjet fighter-bomber squadron MAG22.

On his first mission on an objective near Pyongyang in North Korea, he managed to drop his bombs. Then he felt the controls tighten. "I knew I'd lost my hydraulic system, but that wasn't as bad as when the entire electrical system went out on me," he said.

A "May Day" call produced no results because his radio was inoperative. So were his fuel and speed gauges. Williams could have bailed out. But he knew he was over enemy territory, and he felt his chances of ever pulling on another Red Sox suit would be dim indeed if he fell among the North Koreans. Besides, he was so tall that he was afraid his legs would jam in the cockpit if he attempted to eject. Finally he picked up another Pantherjet and followed it in. "I didn't know my plane was on fire. If I had, I damn well would have shot the canopy and jumped, long legs or no long legs."

He careened into the field at 200 miles an hour with a bad landing stick. He beat the flames out of the craft to the ground.

The next day he was back on duty.

Williams flew 38 missions in South Korea before being released, and rejoined the Sox on July 29, 1953. But first he had dropped in on the all-star game in Cincinnati fifteen days earlier. Pandemonium struck when the crowd and players spotted the returning hero.

"Hey, Muscles, you ain't changed a bit," said Yogi Berra of the Yankees.

"Oh, boy," Williams said with a mock sigh. "It's Yogi. Now I know I'm home."

He embraced Lou Boudreau, the Red Sox manager. A voice came from the crowd: "Welcome home, Ted." It was Casey Stengel. "I'm proud to shake your hand," said Stengel, "because I'm proud of the job you did in Korea and proud of what you always meant to our league."

"Brother," said Williams, in as friendly a mood as ever in his life, "this is living."

120

So Williams, reclining in his digs in the Somerset Hotel on Commonwealth Avenue in Boston in September of 1957, had some memories that went well beyond baseball.

He pondered, too, the return he had made in 1953 for a .407 average and 13 home runs in just 37 games. From then on he was in stride. He hit .349, had 29 home runs and batted in 89 runs in 1954. The next season produced a .356 average, 28 home runs and 83 RBI. In 1956 he stroked .345, with 242 homers and 82 runs batted in.

And now it was 1957 and he had a chance to win it all at age thirty-nine, and he was flat on his back fighting a virus bug.

Chapter Eleven

"Ted can hit to left when he wants to, he can hit to right, and he can take pretty good aim at them centerfield seats."

Casey Stengel

Mantle went into New York's Lenox Hill Hospital on September 6, not with "sympathy pains" for rival Williams but for treatment of torn ligaments around his left ankle.

Williams was released from confinement on September 9. He was still weak and not at all sure when he could even try to play again. He came back to Fenway Park September 12 for his first workout. It didn't work. He had a relapse the next day. Another examination showed he could start practicing again, but doctors cautioned him not to overdo it.

Kansas City's Athletics, now playing under Harry Craft, who had replaced Boudreau, came to Boston September 17. Ted worked out before the game. "I can pinch-hit if you need me," he told manager Higgins.

Hig took him at his word. He called on Williams in the eighth inning with a man on base and the Sox trailing by two runs. Ted promptly picked a 2-ball, 1-strike pitch by Tom Morgan for his 34th home run. It tied the score and the Red Sox went on to win, 9-8.

He was walked intentionally in a pinch-hitting role September 18 at Yankee Stadium. Whitey Ford would have been better off if he, too, had handed Williams a pass two days later.

Ford always was difficult for Williams: "He had that hard stuff and kept the ball low and outside on me." But with a 2-2 count, Whitey made the mistake of throwing Ted a high fastball.

"It was the only one he ever gave me, the little rat," Williams chortled after delivering it into the right-field seats for a home run, his only one ever off Ford. "And the only reason he put the pitch there at all was because he was tired and had lost a good deal of his control."

Ford, for his part, was so upset he gave up three more runs before Stengel could get in a relief pitcher.

Williams didn't need that home run to make a believer out of Stengel. He had done that long before. Stengel had been one of the first to abandon the shift against Williams. "I'm convinced he can hit to left if you leave it open," Casey said of Ted. "So what's the sense? Ted can hit to left when he wants to, he can hit to right and he can take pretty good aim at them centerfield seats.

"Say, he's not bad, either, when he gets on second base and starts operating on stealing those numbers from the catchers. People don't know that about Williams, but I understand he's better than a fair hand at tipping off those pitches to his friends up at bat. That could be why some of those fellows are getting home runs."

Nor did Stengel's prodigious protégé, Mantle, ever evince anything but the highest admiration for Williams. "I don't think I consciously imitated any other player or athlete," Mantle says today. "But I guess I did try to acquire the general attitude of one other man. That was Ted Williams.

"Ted showed me what it meant to be aggressive up there. He was the best I ever saw. Boy, when he swung, it wasn't any patty-cake, it was like he was out to *destroy* the ball.

"It might not be that way for every batter, but it was that way for Ted and me."

Unquestionably any extraordinary performance in Yankee Stadium was an added thrill for Ted. For some reason, he was forever being called upon to defend his hitting in the Bronx ballyard. Once he had braced Joe Reichler of the Associated Press for writing that he could not hit in Yankee Stadium. "I found out later," said Reichler, "that Ted was a lot closer to being correct than I was. And it was the beginning of a long friendship."

Records show that for his entire career, Williams hit .309 in Yankee Stadium. He played in 158 games there. He went to bat 475 times with 147 hits. He also averaged well over a walk per game in Yankee Stadium.

But the legend—or, more properly, the myth—spread that Yankee Stadium was a hex on him. Even Ted's good friend and business agent Fred Corcoran kidded him about it.

One night at dinner in New York, Corcoran said, "You know, Ted, you remind me of Sam Snead and the U.S. Open. Before the Open, Sam's always as loose as ashes. He shakes hands and you can hardly feel it. But once the Open starts, Sam gets so tight he almost breaks your hand when he shakes it."

Williams was smiling as his garrulous Irish friend went

on. "That's you in Yankee Stadium, Ted. You squeeze the bat so hard it looks like you're trying to make sawdust out of it."

"Huh?" said Williams, now poker-faced. "Say, Fred, what did you bat in your day?"

That closed the subject, if only for the time being, Corcoran's irrepressibility being what it is.

Ted's pinch-homer off Ford had given him an eight-point lead over Mantle in the batting race, .374 to .366. The next day, September 21, he was ready to start for the first time since August 31.

Stengel shuddered at the thought. "That old guy looks so much better than anybody else in the league, they better stop thinking about how old he is," said Stengel.

This time Williams was facing Bob Turley. Turley was Williams' meat as a pitcher because basically he just threw hard. The hurler was on a hot streak now and had virtually carried the club for the past month.

Williams first came up against Turley in the second inning. Sammy White, Jim Piersall and Billy Klaus were on base. They did not have to wait long for a free ride home. Williams made contact with a 2-0 Turley pitch and the ball landed in the right-field stands. Williams had the fifteenth grand-slam shot of his career and his 36th home run of 1957.

The Yankees wanted no more of Williams that day. He was walked three straight times. Thus he had three home runs in his last three official times at bat.

Even Yankee fans were booing their own pitchers for walking Williams so steadily. Tom Sturdivant gave Ted a base on balls his first time up September 22, then decided to pitch to him in the fourth.

That was a mistake. Williams rode it out. He had tied a major-league record of four-straight home runs and his total for the season reached 37.

He singled his next time up before the Yankees got the

125

message again. They gave him a pass his last time at bat and his .383 average was 18 points above Mantle's.

The Yankees won that game, 5-1, but they had to wait a day to clinch their 23rd American League championship and their eighth in the last nine years.

The day the Bombers nailed it down, Williams had switched fields from New York to Washington, and his one-man show was not over yet.

Before the Washington game, September 24, he watched young Ralph Lumenti warming up for the Senators. Lumenti was a product of Milford, Massachusetts, near Boston, and Williams was thinking, "Boy, this guy looks like he may be some pitcher. The Red Sox shouldn't have let him get away."

The feeling was only temporary. He singled off Lumenti, then walked three times and finally was hit by a pitched ball by Dick Hyde.

He had been on base an incredible sixteen times in a row.

Later Williams might say that he had not been cognizant of such things as the sixteen-games-getting-on-base streak. Perhaps he had only forgotten. When a man plays 2,292 games in the major leagues, he is no more likely to remember them all than a grocer who has put in that much time in his store. But when things were current, Ted was cognizant. The few times he overlooked records and streaks, literally hundreds of fans felt it incumbent upon themselves to write and remind him.

So you may make book that Williams knew he had been on base sixteen times in a row when he went to bat in Washington against Hal Griggs in the first inning on September 24.

He advanced upon the plate in long strides, slightly revolving his shoulders to loosen the muscles. With his left foot he carefully scratched out a hole in the ground for a better fit for the heel spikes of that foot. Then, as though performing a ballet routine, he meticulously extended his right foot one yard forward.

Griggs fidgeted on the mound. Ted extended his bat to the far corner of the plate. This seemed to be intended to prove both to himself and the pitcher that his swing would cover the entire plate, so don't get cocky, Hal, old buddy.

Next he flexed his hips and legs. He gripped the bat tightly and ground his hands into the bat first in one direction and then the other. Now he was fully confident that he could handle any good pitch.

The good pitch came. Griggs cut the "gut" of the strike zone with a fastball. Williams swung. His timing was a shade off. He merely topped the ball to the infield and was easily out at first base.

Griggs sighed. Williams glared. An infield out was bad enough. An infield out after reaching base sixteen straight times was far worse.

In the fourth inning, Ted returned to the box. Griggs was not quite so nervous now. He gave Williams the same pitch.

Williams' body came twisting around. His power drove off the left foot. Away went the ball. Home run.

It was his 38th and final homer of the year.

He struck out in the sixth inning and walked again in the eighth. But his average had risen to .384 and he was 18 points ahead of Mantle.

The Red Sox were not finished hitting home runs. Malzone whammed two and Jensen and Piersall one apiece as Boston edged Washington, 7-6. Williams was far from inactive, however, with two singles in three trips in the next-to-last series of the year.

Now it was back to Boston and the finish. The Yankees were coming to town. Pennant-clinching notwithstanding, they were anxious to show Williams they weren't completely duck soup for him. On this occasion they did right well as Williams got nothing in one time at bat in six innings.

In another six-inning stint on September 28, he doubled off Sturdivant in the first inning, walked in the third and was called out on strikes in the sixth.

A crowd of 25,406 paid to see Williams' last performance of 1957. He doubled off Art Ditmar and ripped a single through Joe Collins at first base. The Yankees protested that single should have been an error. To them, it meant that their pitchers' combined earned-run average was 3.000 instead of 2.999 for the season. "The ball went right between Collins' legs," Casey Stengel said sourly.

Small matter. Williams had finished with .388, the highest major-league average since his own .406 in 1941. He had defeated Mantle by 23 points. At thirty-nine he was the oldest man ever to win the batting championship. Closest to him was old Honus Wagner, who was thirty-seven when he won the National League title with .334 in 1911. Nearly a half-century had passed between the two events, and the spread in percentage points between Williams and Wagner was an awesome 54.

The .388 gave Williams his fifth American League hitting crown. His .731 slugging percentage placed him highest in that category for the ninth time, and was the best in the majors since 1941.

He had hit for 307 total bases in 420 times up, made up of 38 home runs, 28 doubles and one triple.

On the facing page is Williams' complete 1957 batting record broken down by teams.

Still, a disappointment awaited him. Williams did not win the Most Valuable Player award for the American League in 1957. He had not won it in 1941, either, when he hit .406.

Against	Games	Season	Home	Road	Day	Night	BB	SO	HR
Cleveland	18	.474	.467	.481	.595	.250	10	17	1
New York	20	.453	.531	.333	.447	.500	20	7	6
Kansas City	21	.433	.464	.406	.390	.526	22	2	3
Detroit	18	.359	.361	.357	.311	.474	16	9	9
Baltimore	18	.348	.333	.359	.333	.375	17	11	6
Chicago	18	.333	.440	.237	.357	.286	13	6	6
Washington	19	.333	.214	.448	.316	.368	22	2	7

He masked his disappointment and said it didn't matter a whole lot. After all, he had been MVP in 1946 and 1949. And he was named *The Sporting News* Major League Player of the Year in 1957.

Mickey Mantle was the MVP. "Well, Mickey was playing on a winning team," said Williams. "And you've got to put the premium on winning. Besides, I got *The Sporting News* award. You can't have everything."

Everyone else did not dismiss it so blandly. It turned out that two members of the Baseball Writers' Association of America had placed Williams ninth and tenth in the balloting.

For the first time in his quarter-century as owner of the Red Sox, Tom Yawkey displayed public outrage. "Incompetent and unqualified to vote," Yawkey said of the two dissidents.

It was established that the two low votes for Williams had *not* come from Boston, but out of other American League cities. The votes of the three Boston selectors were revealed:

Hy Hurwitz, *Globe*:
1—Gil McDougald, Yankees.
2—Williams
3—Roy Sievers, Washington.

129

4—Mantle.
5—Frank Malzone, Red Sox.

Joe Cashman, *Record*:
1—Williams.
2—McDougald.
3—Mantle.
4—Nelson Fox, White Sox.
5—Sievers.

Henry McKenna, *Herald*:
1—Williams.
2—Sievers.
3—Mantle.
4—Vic Wertz, Tigers.
5—Malzone.

Yawkey was steaming, not at Boston journalists but at the unidentified hinterlanders who had put Williams ninth and tenth: "Not to take anything away from Mickey Mantle, whom I admire as a wonderful ballplayer, there are some aspects of the most valuable player award that disturb me. As for the votes for ninth and tenth for Ted Williams, I do not think anyone who lets personalities interfere with his judgment is qualified or competent to vote. . . ."

Even Mantle was aghast. "Gee, I thought Ted would win it easy," he said at the Mayo Clinic in Rochester, Minnesota, where he was undergoing treatment. "I thought I lost my chance for MVP when I missed so much playing time at the end of the season."

Mantle polled six first-place votes of a possible 25 and had a total of 233 points. Williams had five first-place votes and 209 points. Sievers, in third place, was named for first place on four ballots and had 205 points, breathing down Williams' neck.

Record writer Cashman called the voting "inconceivable." McKenna of the *Herald* said he thought "something should be done to rectify the situation."

Curt Gowdy, the Red Sox announcer, said with commendable restraint that he believed New Englanders "would take a very dim view of this MVP vote."

There had been other such occurrences. In 1947 Williams had won the triple crown—batting championship, runs-batted-in championship and home-run championship—but the MVP award had gone to Joe DiMaggio. One Boston selector had not even given Williams a *tenth-place vote*.

What happened in 1957, almost all agreed, was despicable. Wrote Arthur Daley in *The New York Times*:

> Disgraceful. The election never should degenerate into a popularity contest, but the brusque, outspoken Williams has never concealed the contempt which he holds for many of the press-box tenants. This is one way of returning the compliment. . . .
>
> Personal prejudices should have no bearing on an election of this sort. But voters are human and therefore let their emotions influence their reason. It's a shame it had to happen that way.

Jimmy Cannon, New York syndicated columnist, maintained that the vote proved Williams was right in his view of the writers. "Some ball journalists declined to vote for him because they considered him rude and abusive," he said. "They proved Williams was correct when he vilified them as slanderous and prejudiced incompetents."

It was the first such massive journalistic outpouring of

131

sympathy for Ted Williams; and, although he never said as much, he felt it quite deeply.

"I'd known since 1956 that the fans were for me, ever since I was fined $5,000 for spitting." At that time several writers had suggested Williams get out of the game. "Give up on baseball," said Harold Kaese in the *Boston Globe*, "before it gives up on you."

But the next night he heard perhaps the loudest applause of his career. "That ought to prove how the fans feel about me," he said.

From that point on, Williams' popularity climbed, despite another $250 fine for spitting in 1958 and a bat-throwing incident the same year. "The bat slipped out of my hand," said Williams after the stick struck, of all people, Red Sox general manager Joe Cronin's housekeeper, Gladys Heffernan, who never even complained about the incident. That year he won his sixth American League batting title, and his second in a row, with .328.

In 1959, a neck injury contributed to his worst season—a .254 average, 10 home runs and 43 runs batted in—and he swore he had had it.

But his original disgust over such a year soon translated itself into a determination to wipe out the memory of it. So he came back in 1960. In 1960, when he was forty-two years old, Williams hit .316 with 29 home runs and 72 runs batted in.

On June 17, 1960, he hit the 500th home run of his career, and padded that statistic to 521 before he called it quits.

Williams, Mickey Vernon and Early Wynn were the only major-leaguers whose careers spanned parts of the 1930's, 1940's, 1950's and 1960's.

His lifetime batting average by months breaks down this way:

MONTHS	HITS	HOME RUNS	AVERAGE
April	156	31	.333
May	434	94	.335
June	504	99	.336
July	546	107	.354
August	544	101	.341
September	460	88	.358
October	10	1	.500

His lifetime batting record by clubs and parks:

Club	HOME HR	HOME Average	AWAY HR	AWAY Average	TOTAL HR	TOTAL Average
New York	32	.375	30	.309	62	.345
Cleveland	36	.343	43	.302	89	.324
Chicago	31	.352	34	.295*	65	.323
Detroit	33	.332	55	.330	88	.331
Washington	33	.382	23	.325	56	.354
Baltimore	15	.357	5	.301	20	.329
Kansas City	10	.362	15	.371	25	.367
Philadelphia	31	.370	35	.353	66	.361
St. Louis	27	.387	33	.399	60	.393

When he quit playing, he had produced 521 home runs off 224 different pitchers. Sixty-two of those came against left-handers. His chief victims had been some of the best pitchers. Twelve homers came off Virgil Trucks, ten each off Bob Feller and Ned Garver, and eight each off Fred

* Williams hit only .220 in the White Sox park his final four seasons.

Hutchinson and Early Wynn and Jim Bunning.

On January 20, 1966, he was elected to Baseball's Hall of Fame. He made it the first year he was eligible. Necktieless as usual, he listened in Fenway Park to the announcement of his election by the highest number of votes in history. He received 282 votes and was left off only twenty ballots. That gave him 93.3 percent of the total vote. The only higher percentage had been registered by Ty Cobb, who got 226 of 226 votes in 1936.

"I can't tell you how pleased I am," said Williams, smiling but showing no other visible emotion. "I've always known how lucky I've been to be connected with Tom Yawkey and the Red Sox. I'm also convinced I was just as lucky to be in a town with such rabid fans. And I want to thank the writers for making all this possible—the chance to get in in my first year as an eligible. I am very proud of that."

It was a nice way to go after eighteen seasons in a Boston uniform, almost all of those shimmery with brilliance. But 1957, when he cut Father Time down to size, truly was Theodore Samuel Williams' golden year.

Afterword

A millionaire can "retire" at thirty, if he's all that sick of making money. Most others have to plug along until they are sixty-five. Plenty never can afford to retire. For Ted Williams, retirement came at a perfect age. He was forty-two. He had done just about everything he ever wanted to in the field he most wanted to do it, and he had years ahead to do whatever he pleased.

From September 1960, when he put aside his playing uniform for the last time, Williams had eight years to devote to his hobby of fishing. He was financially secure through prior long-term arrangements with Tom Yawkey and the Red Sox. But he made his hobby pay big money as a sporting-goods consultant with Sears Roebuck and Co., a connection he kept even after becoming manager of the

Washington Senators and elevating them to a startling .500-plus record in 1969.

With Sears Ted spent considerable time checking out the company's products, including guns, camping gear, fishing tackle and other such items, and representing Sears at conventions and sales meetings and sports shows. Sears was fully appreciative of the pulling power of Williams' name. For his part, Ted enjoyed both the association and the money.

He still spent the greater part of each year between his Islamorada home in the Florida Keys and his cabin on the banks of the Miramichi River in New Brunswick. He interrupted his sojourns in his two Shangri-las for business trips but little else. He was all but inaccessible to writers, photographers and other people from communications media. Much of his resentment at some Boston writers had still not subsided, nor would it ever. He considered interviews (except for those with close friends of long standing) intrusions upon the time he had for fishing.

As he turned into his fiftieth year, Williams either began to miss baseball more or fishing less, or perhaps both, although the first thesis may be closest to the truth.

In New Brunswick he delighted in fishing for the Atlantic salmon. There he was certain not to be bothered or distracted. His solitude in the Keys was not as full, for his pale concrete-brick-stucco home in Islamorada sat only a block or so off U.S. Highway 1, one of the most congested federal arteries, since it is the only overland route between Miami and Key West.

His telephone number there was concealed with painstaking care. He would not even allow it to be printed on the telephone in the spacious living room of the two-story home by a waterway. To contact him, one had to telephone his combined secretary and answering service, and just getting *that* number was a project. Even when a message was left by a close friend, Ted might be a long time returning it. He considered the home a personal fortress from a prying public and ran it as such. A high chain-link fence surrounded the property. Usually the gate was locked. The house was hidden from public view by exotic varieties of trees and shrubs.

Once he welcomed someone to his castle-fortress-home, though, the welcome was effusive, almost nerve-shattering. That was the sort of greeting we received when a small search party of myself, *Sports Illustrated*'s John Underwood and Miami newspaper photographer Charles Trainor managed to gain admission to the sanctum in mid-1967.

I wanted—had wanted for years—to do a series of articles on Williams for the *Miami Herald*. Underwood was after a story for his magazine, which had long been without anything of a personal nature about No. 9.

Ted met us togged out in battered walking shorts and a T-shirt. Originally perhaps the shorts were a bright red. By the time we saw them, they were faded and smeared from a hundred fishing trips, and the shirt was an off-gray model that resembled the test item for a washing-machine company after several thousand run-throughs.

"Nah, I still don't wear neckties," he said, waving us into the living room. "I still have a few of those phonus-balonus little bow-ties, you know, the kind you clip on. But that's all. Hell, I was years ahead of the time with sport shirts. That's being proven right now by all the people wearing turtlenecks. They're not only more comfortable, they're *prettier!*"

He was employing a day maid to keep the house neat. It was indeed tidy for a single man, as he was at the time, being some months short of his third marriage. He shunned air-conditioning for a large floor fan which stood to the right of the front door as one entered. It blew directly into

137

Williams' face in the easy chair he occupied beside the telephone (I couldn't help but wonder why he sat so close to the telephone when he despised it so).

I happened to be sitting between Williams and the floor fan. I was smoking a cigarette even more repugnant than most to him. After failing to make his point by flailing the air, coughing, sniffling and generally indicating his distaste for the noxious weed, he finally asked if I would mind taking a perch downwind of him. This was to be repeated many times in the next few days between non-smoker Williams and smokers Trainor and myself. "My God!" he would gasp if one of us lit a cigarette more than once an hour, "you're a *chain-smoker!*" It also happened in a restaurant, where it was not so simple to have the fumes wafted completely away from him.

We had arrived in the morning, quite proud at having arisen so early. He, of course, had been up since just past dawn. For hours, as we sat in the large living room, he talked freely of his baseball days. Never in that time did he put down an individual player, but his impressions of moderns in general were not favorable.

"They don't want to pay the price to be great hitters," he said. "But I guess that's just the times, big money, big automobiles, television, so much else to do." He had ample reason to believe this. Occasionally, as part of his "vice-presidential" duties following his active career with the Red Sox, he had been called upon to try to sign young prospects.

"A few years ago," he said, "I went to a kid's house and offered him a $100,000 bonus to sign with the Red Sox. I offered his mother $20,000 on top of that. He turned it down and went on to the University of North Carolina to play football."

He said the boy's name was Ken Willard, who later

138

became a star fullback with the San Francisco 49ers of the National Football League.

"I guess you have to expect it," he said. "A good college football player can figure he only has to play thirty games in college to be ready for the football pros. It isn't that simple in baseball.

"The point I'm making is, the day of the hungry great prospect is just about over. That's one reason baseball has been going down in popularity."

This, remember, was some eighteen months before he finally hearkened to the call of Robert Short and became manager of Short's Washington club on a long-term contract starting with the 1969 season.

We had come to fish with him or, more important, to watch him fish. He suggested we do just that. He was no more able to sit still than he had ever been. As he began fussing about, I told him a trivial story that captured his fancy in a way that later occurred to me as at least one of his reasons for returning to baseball as a manager.

"I have a sixteen-year-old son," I said, "and I told him I was coming down to Islamorada to see Ted Williams. And he said, 'Man, Dad, that's terrific! Ted Williams! That's the guy does all that fishing stuff for Sears!' "

I told Williams, for the sake of grace, that I had informed my son that Ted Williams also had played a game or two of baseball once upon a time.

Williams was enchanted. "No kidding?" he said. "No kidding?" He smiled, frowned, smiled again. Perhaps "intrigued" would be a better word than "enchanted." He could not seem to make up his mind whether he was pleased to be known to youngsters primarily as a fishing expert or disappointed that his baseball image among teenagers was fading after seven years out of the game. "Well," he said finally, "that's the new generation for you. They never heard of Ted Williams the baseball player. You have to live with the times."

Eventually two fishing guides arrived. One was Jack Brothers, originally a Long Islander and now an expert on Keys fishing, and the other was a younger man named Billy Grace. Brothers is an engaging raconteur and he began telling a fancy story about the orca, or killer whale. He had barely finished the tale when Williams stalked to a hall closet and pulled out a thick volume called *Wise Encyclopedia of Fishing*. He wanted to check Brothers' story.

"For crying out loud!" Brothers groused. "A guy tells a fish story and you pull an encyclopedia on him!"

Soon we were deployed in two fishing skiffs off Long Key, about ten miles south of Williams' digs. The fishing was poor. Most of the tarpon, Williams explained, had departed for the inland rivers by this time of June. He spent the better part of an hour debating Brothers on the merits of certain knots. They were constantly at each other. When Brothers asked where the clippers were, Williams retorted heavily, "Right here. Right where they're supposed to be. Oh, aren't we *lucky?* Aren't we *lucky?*"

Brothers told a story about a guide named Cecil Green. "Ol' Cecil had some city fellows out tarpon-fishing," said Brothers, "and they were goofing up everything, and finally Cecil said, 'Gentlemen, be seated. To catch fish, you must present the bait properly. You are presenting it improperly. Gentlemen, there are two ends to a fish. There is the eating end and there is the *other* end. From now on, CAST YOUR BAIT TO THE EATING END!' "

Williams roared. But quickly he went back looking for tarpon. He raised one, but it got off the hook on the first jump.

After two hours Williams directed our party to the back country, on the west side of U.S. Highway 1 away from the

Atlantic Ocean, to an area known as Buchanan Keys. By boat it was a good-sized run, close to thirty minutes. Keys guides have high-powered motors on their skiffs and the guides' kidneys are either immune to the chopping rat-a-tat-tat on the bottoms of the skiffs or they simply affect a nonchalant attitude. In Williams' case, the running between fishing holes is honest enjoyment. He enjoys speed whether it is in a boat or car or airplane. During the next few days he would drive us through the severely narrow Keys bridges at speeds right at the limit and steering only with his knees as he used his hands to make conversational points.

I remember a time in 1950, between his two service tours, when he had taken the controls of a chartered plane bringing the Red Sox from Sarasota to Miami for an exhibition. Other Red Sox had either feigned terror or honestly expressed it, with their temperamental pacemaker at the wheel. Just before the plane landed, Williams bounced from the cockpit and into the passenger section and yelled, "Don't worry, you guys. I'm letting the regular driver take it in."

Finally we were off the Buchanan Keys. We waited another spell for some action. Williams peppered the vacant intervals with questions: "What do you think of Vietnam?" "What kind of fighter is Joe Frazier? Could he beat Cassius Clay?" "Will the University of Miami have a good football team this year?"

Constantly he questioned photographer Trainor on exposures and meter-settings and other photographic expertise. "I had a guy down here once to take a special commercial film of me fishing," he said. "I'd been fishing all day and finally got this tarpon on the line, and the photographer just sat there staring. I finally caught the fish and the guy didn't have anything on film. I had to run him off. I don't understand people like that."

141

Darkness was closing in when the tarpon began shaking themselves out of the mud and running along a sandbar. In quick succession Williams had three tarpon on his hook. "When they run by here," he had warned, "you might see a flash that looks orange or black. You only see about 1/20th of the fish."

His first tarpon off the Buchanan Keys quicksilvered out of the water, angrily flung its head and was gone. "Spit out the bucktail!" Williams grimaced. "Nothing you can do about that."

The second tarpon hit hard. Almost too quickly to see, Williams pumped the rod upward three times. Then it was pump-pump-pump to the side, a swishing sound like three knives whirring through the air. The fish went into the air a half-dozen times as Ted played it around the boat. "When they act like they're going under you, you better loosen the drag in a hurry," he said, still manipulating the rod. But this one also got away.

We parked the boats at the fishing camp and began the harrowing drive back up the highway. Regretfully I am unable to recount exact quotations on the return trip, as Williams' knees-against-the-steering-wheel technique distracted me past hearing what was said, or caring. After a while he pulled off on the right side of the highway less than a mile from his home.

"Great little restaurant," he said, pointing. The small sign read MANNY AND ISA'S. Williams explained that they were Cubans, and Manny had been the chef at the more pretentious Green Turtle Restaurant down the road before he went out on his own. By contrast with the Green Turtle, Manny and Isa's is tiny. But it is immaculate, and both owners clearly are enamored of Williams.

"Mister Ted!" cried Isa, the vivacious wife. She nodded enthusiastically at his friends who looked as scruffy as Williams did.

142

He had a beer, for the thirst of a day's fishing. He ordered black beans and rice with onions, and turtle steak for all. Williams does not insist that you eat what he eats but it always seems to wind up that way. "Besides," he said, "you'll never get better turtle steak than you will here." He waited until Isa was well out of hearing before he said that.

When Isa brought out the turtle steak, he winked around the table. "There's a rumor around," he said loudly, making certain several nearby parties could hear, "that a certain restaurant in the Keys is serving *veal* and calling it *turtle steak*." Turtle steak has a definite veal flavor but at the same time a piquancy lacking in veal. "Now I'm not naming any names, but . . ." Innocently he looked down at his plate.

"You stop that, Mister Ted," Isa said in mock anger. "I will take you back into the freezer and show you this is turtle steak. . . ."

Williams looked up with a blank expression. "Who said anything about this place?" He resumed eating as Isa threw up her arms and walked away.

It was nearly 11 P.M. when we left the restaurant. "We want to catch that same tide," he said. "We'll meet at my house for breakfast at five o'clock and be out at Buchanan by seven."

So we met at his house, groggy. He was already making breakfast. Attempts to help were met with presumed outrage. "Just set your behinds in those chairs and keep out of the way," he warned.

A cat was yowling outside the door by the time breakfast was over. "Damned cat," said Williams. "I hate 'em. I chunked a few coconuts at that one one night to try to run him off, but he just sat there and watched the coconuts go by."

Williams walked to the kitchen door with a platterful of

leftover bacon. "Get the hell out of the driveway!" he shouted at the cat. Then he leaned over and set the bacon in front of the cat. "Might as well give it to him as waste it," he said sheepishly.

By nine-thirty that morning, Williams had his tarpon, a 95-pounder.

The photographer got the picture. Williams told him what setting to use.